S0-CBI-861

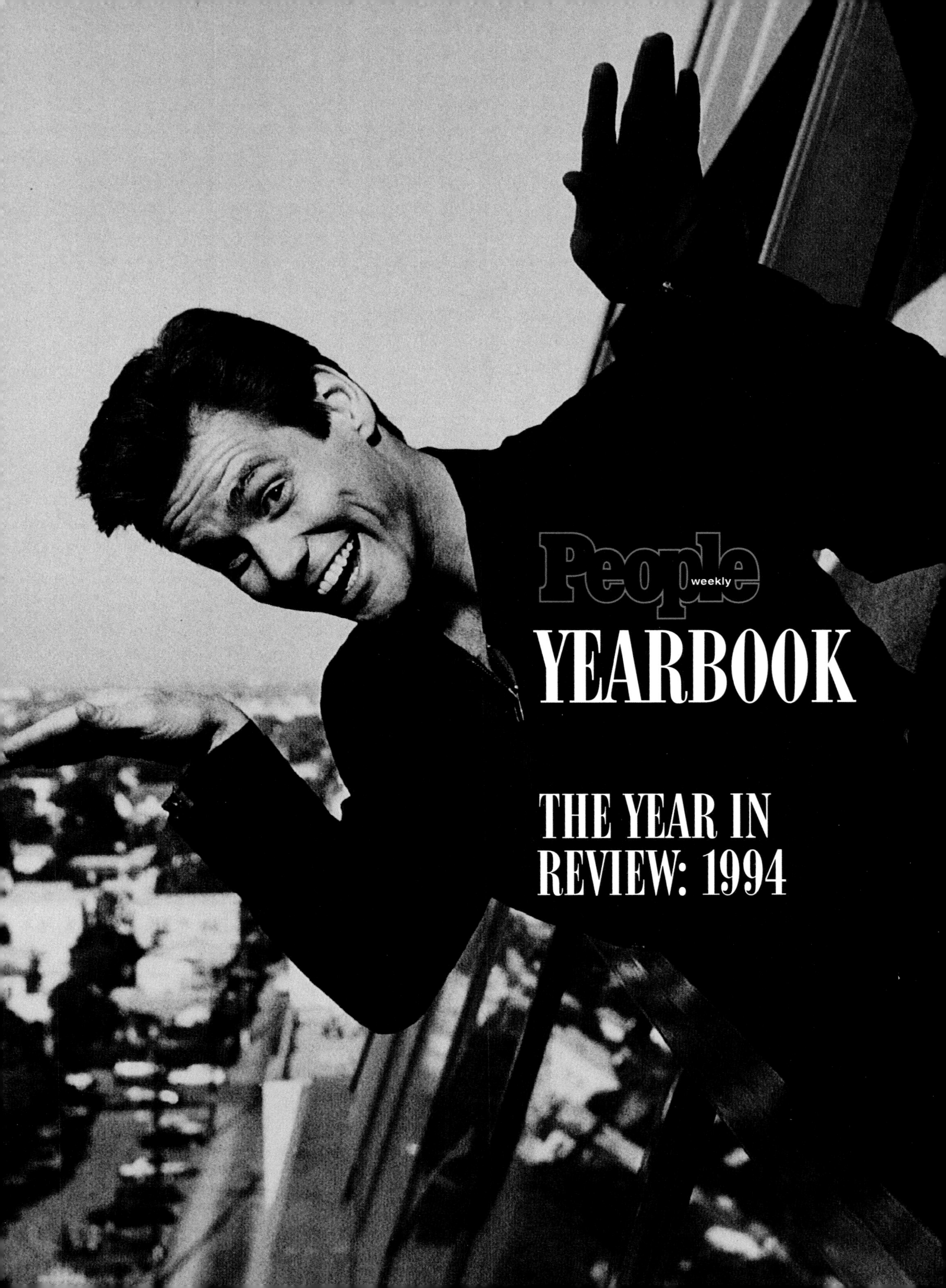
People weekly
YEARBOOK
THE YEAR IN
REVIEW: 1994

Published by

A division of Time Inc. Home Entertainment
1271 Avenue of the Americas
New York, NY 10020

ISBN: 1-883013-04-6
Manufactured in the United States of America

PEOPLE YEARBOOK 1995

Special thanks to Alan Anuskiewicz, Sarah Brennan-Green, Robert Britton, Deirdre Cossman, Jennifer De Luca, Brien Foy, Mary Ellen Lidon, Mary Carroll Marden, James Oberman, Sarah Rozen, Matthew Semble, Freyda Tavin, Alison Sawyer, Ricki Tarlow, Maria Tucci and, for the introductory essay, Richard Lacayo.

CONTENTS

Life was a media circus: Whoopi Goldberg (above) opened the Las Vegas Planet Hollywood in style; cameramen (right) donned Robert Shapiro masks to greet O.J.'s attorney; Prince Charles tried "Terminator" glasses at a trade show, perhaps seeking a rosier scenario; and Michael Fay, the American youth caned in Singapore, sought refuge behind stepfather Marco Chan (far right).

MOMENTS TO REMEMBER

REWIND!

Aflame with lovers, lawyers and lively new luminaries, **1994** *was a year that crackled*

The Victorian poet Matthew Arnold once complained that the problem with America was "a want of the interesting." Okay, maybe the 19th was a slow century. If he had lived to see 1994—a year when John Travolta came back and the World Series didn't, when George Foreman could be heavyweight champ and Howard Stern king of the book world, when Oscar night carried in Whoopi Goldberg as host and Election Day carried out the Democrats—we think we could have changed his mind.

This was a year so absorbing it's hard to believe so much could take place so fast. That whole business with the tough Olympic skater and the nice one who got kneecapped. And the American kid who got caned in Singapore. It does make for a topsy-turvy 12 months when people get hit with sticks too often and baseballs not enough.

And unlike certain snippy British poets, when we turned our attention overseas, we found plenty to amuse us. It was a year, after all, in which Carlos the Jackal, long the world's most diabolical terrorist, was nabbed while report-

edly undergoing liposuction surgery to reduce his tummy. And James Herriot, the best-selling British veterinarian, got trampled by some belligerent sheep. And the students of the august London School of Economics elected Mick Jagger their honorary president. He beat out Carlos the Jackal. No kidding—sometimes not even liposuction will win you a popularity contest.

Above all here was the year in which the arrest and trial of O.J. Simpson nearly overwhelmed the circuits of the national imagination. There's still a line burned down our brains, left there by the image of a Ford Bronco coursing slowly down a highway while a flying wedge of police cars follows in dreamy pursuit. (And we all hover above it, watching TV's copter shot.) What did the Simpson case give us? One more opportunity to revisit the dilemmas of race and domestic violence. A look at state-of-the-art lawyering by Robert Shapiro and the other players in the courtroom. Most usefully, it offered a tragic standard that put less fateful public events in perspective. Were Charles and Diana really such a pitiable couple, or just some badly spoiled sports? Why did Richard Gere and Cindy Crawford take out a full-page ad in *The Times* of London proclaiming their heterosexuality and their commitment to one another, only to publicly announce their separation six months later? Have we known egg timers that took longer to run out than the marriage of Shannen Doherty and Ashley Hamilton? They'll get over it. After all, we did.

Is it sheer strangeness that makes something interesting? Then we give you 1994, the year in which Dennis Franz became a sex symbol and Forrest Gump a font of wisdom. When Wood-

There's still a line burned in our brains, left there by the image of a Ford Bronco...

...on screen it was a year of living dangerously,
off screen you could still find happy endings...

stock II...well, what kind of youthfest has an official refrigerator magnet? Not to mention that steamroller of weirdness, the Fort Knox of secret intentions, the harmonic convergence of strange stuff—the marriage of Michael Jackson and Lisa-Marie Presley. You want interesting? Was there anything in Matthew Arnold's Victorian London to compare with that? Okay, the Elephant Man—but wasn't Michael supposed to have bid on his remains?

There was something else strange about 1994. When it came to movies and television, we seemed to think that the flavorful and the tasteless were one and the same. *Pulp Fiction*, *Natural Born Killers*, the up-close-and-personal view of your large intestine on *ER*—we liked our entertainments to be a bloody ball of contusions. It says something that Oprah Winfrey, who had the stamina to finish her first marathon this year, walked out on a screening of *Interview with the Vampire* when the gore was too much. And you knew it was a rough year when Canadian TV banned the cartoon version of the Mighty Morphin Power Rangers. Even the Lion King ended up as roadkill under a stampede of wildebeests.

If on screen it was a year of living dangerously, off screen you could still find happy endings. Ten years after taking a dive on the charts, Bruce Springsteen bounced back with a songwriting Oscar. The speed skater Dan Jansen caught up with the Olympic gold that escaped him twice before. Ricki Lake,

Frasier's Kelsey Grammer (top) romped with fiancée and third-wife-to-be, Tammi Baliszewski; cutting to the chase (from right, below), Anthony Edwards, Sherry Stringfield and Eriq La Salle made _ER_ the tube's must-watch new series; and Woodstock II stuck to the ribs.

125 pounds lighter than she was a few years before, practically floated upward on the talk show Nielsens. Tracey Gold, who once suffered badly from anorexia, even got to dig into some wedding cake—her own.

Speaking of wedded bliss. Here was the year when Microsoft billionaire Bill Gates finally found the perfect laptop. Pearl Jam's Eddie Vedder found someone to brood with. Rush Limbaugh gained one more sympathetic ear, having met his new third mate via CompuServe. Marla Maples finally got Donald Trump to sign on the bottom line, and even Kelsey Grammer made plans to take the plunge again.

We admit that in 1994 the times became less interesting, too, because we lost some of the people who gave them spice. Grace seems less graceful without Jessica Tandy. Fate less complicated without Richard Nixon. Without Kurt Cobain, youth seems older. Big seems smaller without John Candy. And without Jacqueline Kennedy Onassis, the whole of things seems less than it was. But to make up for their loss, we found new people to appreciate, from Jim Carrey to Sheryl Crow and David Letterman's mom.

How do you sum up a tumultuous year like this? At the Miss America pageant, the winner, Heather Whitestone, managed to make herself perfectly clear in sign language. We've decided to stick with pictures and words to sort it all out. And from our seat in the chopper, it all looked mighty interesting.

The Mighty Morphin Power Rangers (above) trampled Barney in TV and toyland; talk-show Olympian Oprah Winfrey (left), 40, ran her first marathon in commendable time; and Alabama's Heather Whitestone, 26, began her rule as the first deaf Miss America by signing an exuberant "I love you."

...and we loved her, too...

. . . old wounds healed at a sad state occasion . . .

At Richard Nixon's funeral at Yorba Linda, California, five U.S. Chief Executives and their wives grieved together: (from left) the Clintons, the Bushes, the Reagans, the Carters and the Fords. Later in the year, in an affecting, handwritten letter to the nation, Ronald Reagan, 83, revealed that he was suffering from Alzheimer's disease.

. . . in D.C., there were party tricks, party duds, a dramatic change of parties —and a tragic gate crasher . . .

It was a battering year for the White House: The Clinton health-care reform was DOA, and a pilot made a crazed suicide dive (below left). Skewered by the health insurance industry's Harry and Louise TV spots, the First Couple created a parody for a D.C. gathering (far left), while Tipper and the Veep (left) did Halloween. Then, the Republicans took over both houses of Congress, and G.O.P. ideologue Newt Gingrich became the new Speaker of the House—and next in line, after Gore, to the Presidency.

...you can't say *that* on TV!...

Madonna set a tacky tone for '94 on David Letterman's *Late Show*, not only presenting him with a pair of her panties but also rattling off the f word 14 times.

...and politics wasn't the only arena for strange bedfellows.

Former child stars Donny Osmond and Danny Bonaduce (left) duked it out for charity (Danny won); Jordan's King Hussein and Israel's Yitzhak Rabin (above) lit up after signing a peace treaty; Soul Brother No. 1 James Brown (far right) boogied on his 61st birthday with Sex Sister No. 1 Sharon Stone; cross-dresser RuPaul and sexologist Dr. Ruth Westheimer (below right) noshed at a fashion do; while the Duchess of York and Jay Leno (at a benefit) perhaps pondered if they were separated at birth.

chez
C R

HOT PROPERTIES

Some were snappy, some were sexy—from Ricki Lake to **JIM CARREY,** *they all were smokin' in '94*

BRACED FOR FAME AND BUSTIN' OUT

Years ago, when he was just another struggling young comic waiting for his big break, he wrote himself a $10 million check for "acting services rendered" and put it in his wallet. Now he can afford to cash it any time he chooses. With the left-field hit, the $72-million-grossing *Ace Ventura: Pet Detective*, followed by his dizzying star turn in *The Mask*, the irresistible package of rubber limbs, lips, hips known as Jim Carrey is rolling in bucks and boffo notices.

Although critics howled derision at *Pet Detective*, Carrey, 32, became Hollywood's goofiest marquee miracle. He now commands somewhere between $7 million and $10 million per picture, which beats the luminous likes of Daniel Day-Lewis, Anthony Hopkins or Liam Neeson. "He's like Bill Murray was in the '80s," says Peter Farrelly, who directed Carrey in the new comedy *Dumb and Dumber* (in which he plays a millionaire dimwit in pursuit of his dream girl). "Jim's got the '90s wrapped up. He's the funniest guy around right now."

His story seems as old as comedy. Growing up the youngest of four children in a Toronto suburb, where his father Percy was a company comptroller and later a manual laborer, Carrey was a quiet, lonely boy. Discovering that he could make friends by getting other kids to laugh, he spent hours in front of the mirror, contorting his face and talking to himself. He also participated in the Carrey family hijinx, led by Dad, which included stuff like butter fights at the kitchen table.

The budding comedian dropped out of school, he says, in 9th grade, and did his first stand-up routine at age 15. By 1985, Carrey, whose specialty was impressions, caught the eye of Rodney Dangerfield. He became the senior comedian's opening act in Las Vegas. Later, Carrey branched out from impressions to more scatological and physical routines. He also won small roles in films, including *Earth Girls Are Easy* and *Peggy Sue Got Married*. Another break in 1989 brought him to the attention of Damon Wayans, and landed him a regular gig on Wayans' TV series, *In Living Color*.

To get where he is today—a $4 million, seven-bedroom estate in trendy Pacific Palisades—Carrey has faced a number of demons. Plagued by nightmares of murdering his parents and severe bouts of depression, he tried everything from conventional therapy and Prozac to colonics and aura work. "I've been to a place I believe is the edge of a nervous breakdown," he once said. "I like it better where I am now."

Carrey also ended his seven-year marriage to aspiring actress Melissa Womer, 34, mother of their 6-year-old daughter, Jane. Womer isn't talking about what went wrong. But as Carrey tells it, she got fed up with the ways success changed him. "Living with me these last couple of years has been like living with an astronaut," he said. "It's like, 'I just came back from the moon. Don't ask me to take out the garbage.' "

For awhile, Carrey was romantically involved with his *Dumber* co-star, Lauren (*Picket Fences*) Holly, 31, also fresh from a messy marital breakup. Meanwhile, he's salting away some of his millions for his daughter's college education, and putting romance on the back burner. "I was married for seven years, and I've just gone through a divorce," Carrey said. "I'm going to be going crazy for awhile."

ALEXI LALAS

With his flying red mane and goatee, defender Alexi Lalas, 24, made a colorful splash on the home squad in soccer's first World Cup held in the U.S. Then, the Michigan-born, guitar-playing rocker hit the history book: He became the first American ever to play in the elite Italian professional league. "I thought I'd fade off into the obscurity of soccer and do some music," he said. "It was impossible to imagine this."

PAUL REISER

Some comedians never seem to get enough. So razor-sharp Paul Reiser, 38, is going for a romance-based, showbiz hat trick. His NBC sitcom, *Mad About You*, resided comfortably in the top 30, his book *Couplehood*—a light look at relationships—was a best-seller, and he worked on his first big-screen starring effort, *Bye Bye Love* (about three divorcing fathers).

Maybe it helps that the love-obsessed Reiser, the son of a New York City health food distributor, has been married to psychotherapist Paula (with whom he shares a Malibu moment at left) for some six years. "Even when we're relaxing and rejuvenating," says Reiser, "I'm thinking, 'Wow! What about an episode where a couple is so tired, they can't even talk to each other!' "

Heather Locklear

With her gossamer hair and sun-kissed smile, Heather Locklear, 32, is America's Babe Emeritus, hotter now than when she put the nasty in *Dynasty* a decade ago. This year, she helped *Melrose Place* become prime time's naughtiest indulgence and shifted partners off screen. Divorced from Mötley Crüe percussionist Tommy Lee after some eight years of marriage, she became engaged to Bon Jovi lead guitarist Richie Sambora.

Simba the Lion

His roar at the box office sent major studios scrambling for cartoon characters. And no wonder. Likely to gross more than $300 million in ticket sales, *The Lion King*'s Simba may eventually earn Disney Studios more than $1 billion in profits when licensed products and video rentals are totalled. That would make it the biggest money maker in movie history.

KENT NAGANO

Surf's up, and so is third generation Japanese-American conductor Kent Nagano, 42. Anointed the "next Bernstein" for his podium panache, he is based with classical pianist wife Mari Kodama, 27, in San Francisco, but directs orchestras in three countries, has cut 20-plus albums and relaxes by hanging 10 in France.

SHERYL CROW

Singer-songwriter Sheryl Crow, 30, is on the wing: Her debut album, *Tuesday Night Music Club*, cracked *Billboard*'s Top 40, and the single "All I Wanna Do" was Top 10-bound. Her moody melodies echo her own bouts of depression. Says she: "I think we're at a time when people want the real deal."

LUCKY VANOUS

A former Army Black Beret, model Lucky Vanous, 33, was 1994's pop-top phenom. As a shirtless object of desire in a diet Coke commercial (above), he weakened the knees of female channel surfers. And they are thirsty for more. Married to model Kristen Noel, 28, the 6' 2", 190-lb. Vanous exults, "Everyone in America is sitting on their couches waiting for the next one."

Toni Braxton

Her mother taught cosmetology, but soulful pop singer Toni Braxton, 26, couldn't sample the goodies until age 15, when her strict Pentecostal parents let her slide lip gloss around her klieg-light smile. In '94, those lips (and those pipes) set the music world on its ear. Her eponymous CD reached No. 1 and resulted in a slew of Grammys and other awards. "Her charm," says Antonio Reid, co-owner of LaFace, the label for which she records, "is that she is a simple, earthy person." The Severn, Maryland, native keeps the dating game elemental as well. "I judge all men by how they treat their mothers," says Braxton. "But they can't be mama's boys."

Cynthia McFadden

The verdict is in: Journalist Cynthia McFadden, 37, was such a hit on cable's Court TV network covering the Menendez brothers' trial et al that ABC raided her away as law-and-justice correspondent. Hot beat aside, McFadden remains true to her bucolic Maine roots: She favors duds from L.L. Bean and when excited spouts phrases like "Oh, doggies!"

MARGARET CHO

No wonder Margaret Cho, 25, striking a glam pose at right, is laughing. After all, the Korean-American veteran of stand-up clubs got her own ABC show. *All-American Girl* is the first network series with a primarily Asian-American cast. *Girl's* humor reflects Cho's own cross-cultural upbringing in San Francisco. "Growing up," she quips, "I thought that *Kung Fu* with David Carradine should have been called *That Guy's Not Chinese!*"

DAVID HASSELHOFF

Go ahead, call it *Babewatch*—but the series about a group of lifeguards is the most-watched TV show on Planet Earth, regularly viewed by some 1 billion people in 140 countries. So *Baywatch* star and executive producer David (*Knight Rider*) Hasselhoff, 42, is having the last laugh. "All those guys who wouldn't talk to me before come over to me now," he says gleefully. Oh, yes, the father of daughters aged 2 and 4 is also a singer, phenomenally popular in Europe.

Hugh Grant

The fates were not kind to Hugh Grant. They were extravagant. They gave him charm, talent, an Oxford education, a choirboy complexion and a vermouth-dry wit. The engaging 33-year-old Londoner, who plays a bounding bachelor in the surprise hit romantic comedy *Four Weddings and a Funeral*, is a fresh hybrid of Cary Grant and David Niven. Women—and critics—from Tallahassee to Tokyo hail him for reinventing the intelligent, comic leading man. Even Madonna badgered him—unsuccessfully—for a date. He prefers the company of Elizabeth Hurley, 29, his English actress-girlfriend of seven years. Said *Weddings* director Mike Newell: "I haven't found an American woman yet who hasn't flipped for him."

Rosie Daley

Author-chef Rosie Daley gained a best-selling cookbook by helping TV's weight-loss champ (with her in Chicago, at left) drop 72 lbs. in eight months with low-fat, low sugar meals. In fact, *In the Kitchen with Rosie*—thanks in part to Oprah Winfrey's unabashed plugs on her show—became the fastest-selling hardback in history. Daley, 32, who is divorced and has a 12-year-old son who lives with his father in California, found her calling by following her gravel-pit owner dad's advice. "If you cook," he said, "you don't have to do dishes."

WINSTON GROOM

Alabaman Winston Groom, 51, was an esteemed but never forest-leveling novelist until Tom Hanks's smash adaptation of *Forrest Gump*. Soon, 1.2 million paperbacks of the '86 tome hit the shelves, as well as a collection of *Gumpisms*; yes, a sequel is under way.

RALPH FIENNES

In *Schindler's List*, he was an evil Nazi; in *Quiz Show*, British actor Ralph Fiennes (pronounced Rafe Fines), 31, was ethically delinquent Charles Van Doren. Either way, he mesmerizes audiences. "He doesn't say a hell of a lot," notes *Quiz* costar Christopher McDonald. "But when he opens his mouth, he's got 'em."

BRETT BUTLER

To get from a Georgia trailer park to her ABC hit, *Grace Under Fire*, stand-up comic Brett Butler, 36, dropped 40 lbs., had breast enhancement surgery and bleached her hair. She also divorced an abusive husband—which provided her series' bitter back story.

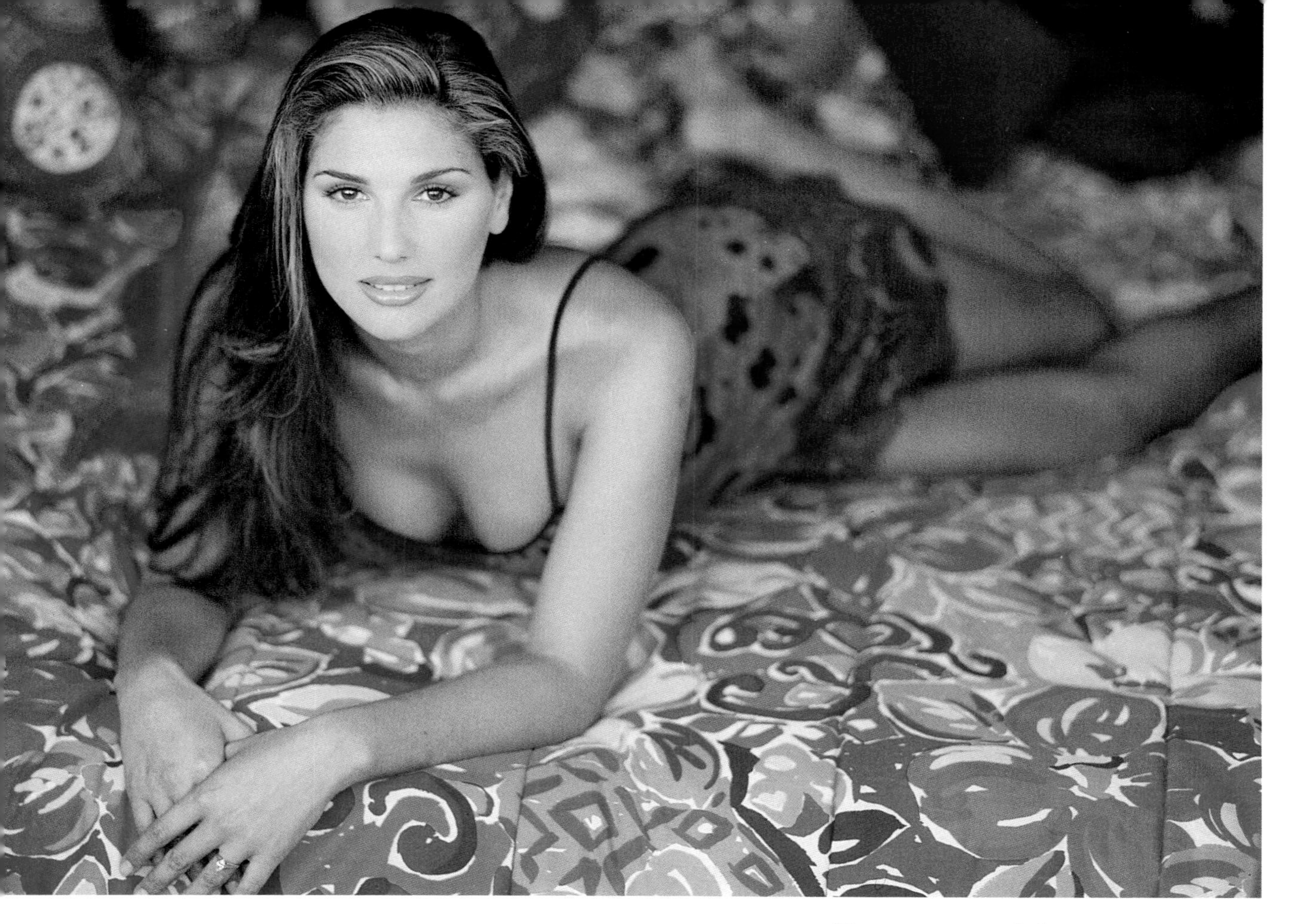

Daisy Fuentes

Born in Cuba and raised in Spain and New Jersey, Daisy Fuentes, 27, has proved the perfect telegenic veejay for MTV's vast global footprint. Her striking Latina looks landed her a Revlon cosmetics contract alongside Cindy Crawford, and in February she began a talk show, *Daisy*, on cable's CNBC, where Phil and Geraldo also gab. Finally, she is part owner of a Manhattan vegetarian restaurant called, appropriately, Dish.

John Michael Montgomery

His looks and his voice had female country fans shivering in their Tony Lamas. John Michael Montgomery, 29, also iced the charts. His two No. 1 CDs and three Top 5 hits earned him two CMA awards this year. And forget the handsome stuff. Says he: "I've got a beer belly, and I'm bowlegged as hell." Sounds like a country song.

Tiger Woods

By age 15, Eldrick "Tiger" Woods was a golfing wonder with more than 100 local titles. But it was in '94, at 18, that the Stanford freshman topped himself, becoming the youngest person to bag the prestigious United States Amateur title, and the first black to do so. Close to his family, and girlfriend Dina Gravell, Woods says, "My priorities are family first, school second, golf third. We're not going to change that."

Doris Kearns Goodwin

With the temporary evanescence of David Caruso, Harvard historian Doris Kearns Goodwin, 51, emerged as the media's most ubiquitous redhead. *No Ordinary Time*—her extraordinary account of Franklin and Eleanor Roosevelt's White House—followed her masterful works on Lyndon Johnson and the Kennedy family. She also proved herself a TV utility infielder with her wise social commentary on *MacNeil-Lehrer* and her affecting reminiscences about bonding with the Brooklyn Dodgers and her dad on the Ken Burns documentary *Baseball*. She is married to former Kennedy speechwriter Richard Goodwin, 62, who wrote the book on which the film *Quiz Show* is based and whose role in it was played by Rob Morrow.

RICKI LAKE

Talk about weight loss. And keep talking. Ricki Lake, 26, the 5' 4", 250-lb. star of John Waters' 1988 comedy *Hairspray*, shed 125 lbs. and gabbed her way to the top. *Ricki Lake* is the No. 2 TV talk show (right behind *Oprah*). Lake also got married to Rob Sussman, 27, a New York City illustrator. The couple met at a Halloween party, fell immediately in love, and, confides Ricki, "we were naked two hours later."

PEOPLE'S 25 MOST INTRIGUING LIST OF 1994

Gerry Adams, 46, *Sinn Fein leader*
Andre Agassi, 24, *tennis ace*
Tim Allen, 41, *actor*
Aldrich Ames, 53, *CIA turncoat*
Nadja Auermann, 23, *fashion model*
Jim Carrey, 32, *comedian*
Vinton Cerf, 51, *Internet cofounder*
Bill Clinton, 48
Diana, Princess of Wales, 33
Shannon Faulkner, 19, *student*
Michael Fay, 19, *whipping boy*
Newt Gingrich, 51, *Speaker of the House-designate*
Tonya Harding, 24, *figure skater*
Whitney Houston, 31, *singer*
Michael Jordan, 31, *baseball player*
Jeffrey Katzenberg, 44, *studio cofounder*
Ricki Lake, 26, *talk-show hostess*
Heather Locklear, 33, *actress*
Mighty Morphin Power Rangers, *TV characters*
Pope John Paul II, 74
Liz Phair, 27, *singer*
James Redfield, 44, *author*
O. J. Simpson, 47
John Travolta, 40, *actor*
Christine Todd Whitman, 48, *Governor of New Jersey*

LUIS MIGUEL

Mexico's spiciest pop import, Luis Miguel, 24, brought his brand of Latin love songs and hip-shaking moves to sold-out U.S. arenas. His *Segundo Romance* hit the American charts at No. 29, one of the highest debut Spanish-language albums ever. Tapped to sing with Sinatra on *Duets II*, Luis has, says producer Phil Ramone, "the kind of pizzazz that comes around only once a decade."

THRIVING LEGENDS

"Just remember," *Peanuts* creator Charles Schulz has quipped, "once you're over the hill you begin to pick up speed." In 1994, a troupe of ageless classics proved that the adage had legs—and lungs, and vision—by zooming to the top again. The golden oldies collected here wowed the MTV generation as well as entrancing their own set with their luminescence and their longevity. For some reason, a society fixated on youth and forward spin took the time to look back over its shoulder and discover that what was old was still fresh. These artists still had show business's ultimate Midas touch—that of class.

Johnny Cash (above), 62, triumphantly twanged in the nation's rock arenas to sell-out crowds; Tony Bennett (left), 67, copped his fourth Grammy for crooning standards and *jammed on MTV's* Unplugged; *Robert Redford (below), 57, directed the critically acclaimed* Quiz Show.

Back on stage after a 22-year absence, Barbra Streisand, 52, wowed her claque, as well as new fans, who shelled out as much as $1,000 a ticket in 13 cities across the country to pay homage to the pipes—and the personality—that headlined the '60s and '70s. And the unstoppable Stones (Mick is 51), their dressing room redolent of Ben-Gay, rolled relentlessly on with Voodoo Lounge, *their 12th U.S. tour in 30 years of ruling rock-n-roll.*

A CIA turncoat was nabbed, sexual harassment was an issue, and **O.J. SIMPSON** *led us on a compelling chase after the nature of guilt and innocence*

THE PEOPLE VS. A PUBLIC HERO

Every decade has its compelling public crime that focuses our fears and passions: the Lindbergh baby kidnapping, the Diet Doctor murder, and the Manson Family massacre, among others. For the '90s, it was the savage stabbing of Nicole Simpson. The Simpson saga had the elements of classical tragedy—as interpreted by *L.A. Law*. O.J. himself was the great figure brought low: a football idol, a role model who seemed to sidestep all the obstacles of society and run to daylight. Yet the great athlete, film actor and TV commercial exemplar couldn't slip past the dark grasp of fate. His eerie low-speed yardage on the freeways of the nation's Dream Capital became a hurdle into history.

Accused of brutally murdering his ex-wife, Nicole Brown Simpson (right), and her friend Ronald Goldman (left), O.J. presented us with more social, emotional, legal and ethical subplots than *Othello*. In a gelid mixture of the tragic and the tawdry, he was variously seen as a jealous wraith, a spousal abuser whose actions raised questions about black on white crime, a victim of racial injustice and an astonishing example of hubris.

His was a case of primal passions in prime time. O.J. was his *own* TV movie, promising revelations of celebrity, high living, money, sex, power and drugs. Court TV and CNN became our Greek chorus, singing woefully of high estate and falls from grace. The drama itself was soaked in stagecraft—bloody footprints, a leather glove, a stocking cap and DNA, the very stuff of our being. Would the last act of this drama provide us with a classical catharsis, a release of pity and fear for the whole of society? No one knew, but everyone stayed tuned. One reason for our rapt attention was a cast of characters, presented on these pages, that never failed to entrance us.

DEFENDING A ROLE MODEL

On defense: some of America's heaviest artillery. In addition to Alan Dershowitz and F. Lee Bailey, who advised from behind the scenes, Team O.J. included jury-selection guru Jo-Ellan Dimitrius (far left), 40, and Johnnie L. Cochran Jr. (standing), 57, a magnetic civil rights lawyer who helped clear football player-turned-actor Jim Brown of rape charges and helped craft Michael Jackson's $15 million child-molestation settlement. Lead lawyer Robert Shapiro (above, and seated below), 52, is Hollywood's A-list attorney. A smooth negotiator, he has represented the likes of Johnny Carson (drunk driving) and Christian Brando (manslaughter). Shapiro met his wife, former model Linell Thomas, in a nightclub. They have two children, Grant, 10, and Brent, 14.

ON THE BENCH

Superior court magistrate Lance Ito, 44, is a second-generation Japanese-American used to the limelight: He sentenced savings-and-loan swindler Charles H. Keating Jr. to prison for securities fraud. Ito raised eyebrows when, after warning both sides about leaks to the press, he himself gave a lengthy interview to an L.A. TV station. He also came under fire from the defense, which raised questions of conflict of interest. Ito is married to LAPD Captain Margaret York, 53, the highest-ranking woman on the force. She was part of a previous investigation of Mark Fuhrman, the detective who found blood spots on O.J.'s Bronco.

FOR THE CITY

Marcia Clark, 41, the combative Deputy District Attorney who leads the L.A. courtroom team, went toe-to-toe with Shapiro & Co. and held her own. The twice-divorced Clark has prosecuted 20 murder cases, winning the 1991 conviction of Robert Bardo, stalker and killer of 21-year-old TV actress Rebecca Schaeffer. Clark is considered an expert on DNA testing and circumstantial evidence, the twin hearts of the O.J. case.

THE TRAGIC SURVIVORS

The murders of Simpson and Goldman left their families grieving—and questioning. O.J. attended his wife's funeral with their children Justin (left), 6, and Sydney, 8. (He has two grown children by first wife Marguerite Whitley.) Now in the legal custody of Nicole's parents, the kids know their mother has "died and gone to heaven," according to a family friend, but not that their father is in jail. The children were sleeping in their mother's condominium when she and Goldman were murdered.

THE ONLY WITNESS

Although officials had the gory pictures of the scene, the DNA scrapings, the hair samples and that singular bloody glove to argue over and speculate about, there was only one survivor who witnessed the crime. It was Nicole's agitated Akita, Kato—whose bloody paw prints were tracked about the bodies of his mistress and her friend—and who led neighbors to the horror on South Bundy.

What Took So Long?

Beginning in 1985, CIA officer Aldrich Ames, 53, stuffed plastic trash bags with classified documents and handed them off to the KGB. This information was responsible for the deaths of as many as 10 key Russian agents who worked for U.S. intelligence. Yet, incredibly, it took nine long years for the Agency to uncover his treason—a failure that shook the spook biz. During that time, Ames pocketed nearly $3 million from the Soviets, which sustained a lavish lifestyle of a magnificent home, a luxury car and Filipino servants.

Though tried and imprisoned for life for his crimes (his Colombian-born wife and co-conspirator, Rosario, 42, drew a five-year sentence), Ames was never reprimanded in a 32-year career, in which he was "sloppy and inattentive," as CIA investigators put it. Fond of liquid lunches, he was once found by Italian police dead drunk in a Roman gutter, and his home computer held drafts of memos to his KGB handlers. "One could almost conclude," said shaken CIA director James Woolsey, "that not only was no one watching, no one cared." Meanwhile, the Ameses' son Paul, 5, lives with his grandmother in Colombia. Before Rosario's sentencing, the boy sent a crayon drawing to the judge, reading, "Judge: Please make mommy come home fast. I love her, Paul."

"He told me, 'Don't ever sign your mind over to someone else. Have some integrity,' " says a school pal of Ames (seen in custody last February).

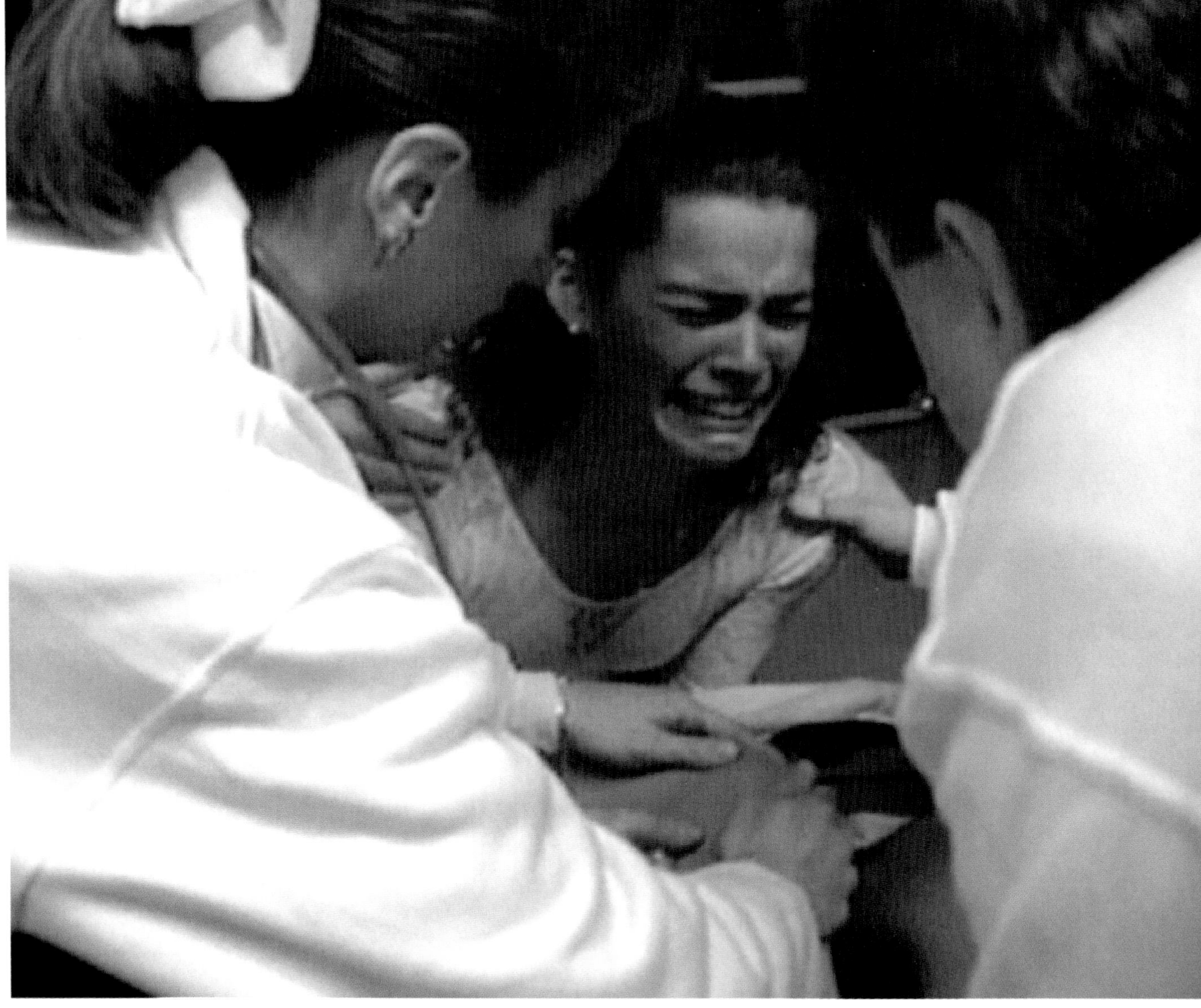

Kerrigan was anticipating a national championship in January until she got bludgeoned on the knee in Detroit.

THE CRUELEST ICE CAPADE

When a shadowy figure struck Nancy Kerrigan on the knee with a metal bar at the U.S. national championships in Detroit's Cobo Arena, she fell to the ice crying, "Why me? Why now? Why?" The answers raised even more questions—what about the hermetic world of championship figure skating, the do-or-die financial stakes of athletic competition, and, ultimately, the very human nature of envy? Although Kerrigan, 24, the U.S.'s brightest hope for Olympic gold, recovered from her injuries to take second place at the Lillehammer, Norway, Winter Games, and Tonya Harding, 23, placed eighth, the sport—even the Games themselves—seemed tarnished and diminished.

Rivals on the ice and off, the two women seesawed their way to the top. Tonya was the 1991 U.S. champion, but by '94, Nancy was America's premier woman skater. At the '92 Games, Kerrigan won a bronze; Harding did not take home a medal. This time, Harding had said, "I'm going to whip her butt."

Away from the arenas, Kerrigan was the sweetheart of the skating establishment with a sparkling smile and a nurturing, working-class family. Tonya, on the other hand, was skating's Pete Rose, a woman whose life and career were dicier. Her mother, LaVona, was a waitress who married untold times. Tonya's father, Al, the fifth husband, left the family when Tonya was 15. LaVona was Tonya's costume seamstress and sharpest critic, sometimes using slaps and punches to improve her daughter's skating.

An unhappy teenager at home in Portland, Oregon, Harding married Jeff

Gillooly, a warehouse worker, in 1990. Fifteen months later she filed for divorce. "I recently found out he bought a shotgun," read her petition to the court, "and am scared for my safety." Within months of the decree, however, the couple reconciled, and the live-in ex-husband resumed his control over Tonya's career. With the help of Tonya's hulking, loud-mouthed bodyguard Shawn Eckardt, Gillooly hired a pair of Portland toughs for $6,000 to incapacitate Tonya's Olympic rival. Within weeks of the attack, Eckardt had confessed to authorities, and a trapped Gillooly fingered Tonya. Prosecutors deferred Harding's trial until after the Games, and the U.S. Olympic Committee allowed her to skate. When she was later found guilty of covering up the plot and hindering the prosecution, she was banned from amateur skating for life.

Since then, Kerrigan, who had grown a thicker skin and a sharper edge from the incident, landed a $1 million deal with Disney and some $11 million in endorsements. She was seeing her newly

With a glance that spoke volumes (right), Harding watched her rival's Olympic warm-up in Norway. Her garrulous bodyguard, Shawn Eckardt (below), had been part of the plot.

divorced manager, ProServ marketing president Jerry Solomon.

Harding, meanwhile, who is involved with Doug Lemon, another warehouse worker, mowed lawns as part of her probation requirement to hold a regular job. Tonya used her notoriety to hype wrestling matches, sell the TV rights to her life story and act in a low-budget flick, in which she plays a feisty waitress fleeing the Mob. She is considering skating professionally in Greece and Japan. "I'm trying to put things back together," Harding said. "I do see a psychiatrist to try and help me through, because it was a tragedy what has happened." The incident haunts Kerrigan as well. "I would like to know how she could do it, but I don't think there's an answer," Nancy said. "I think she needs help in her head."

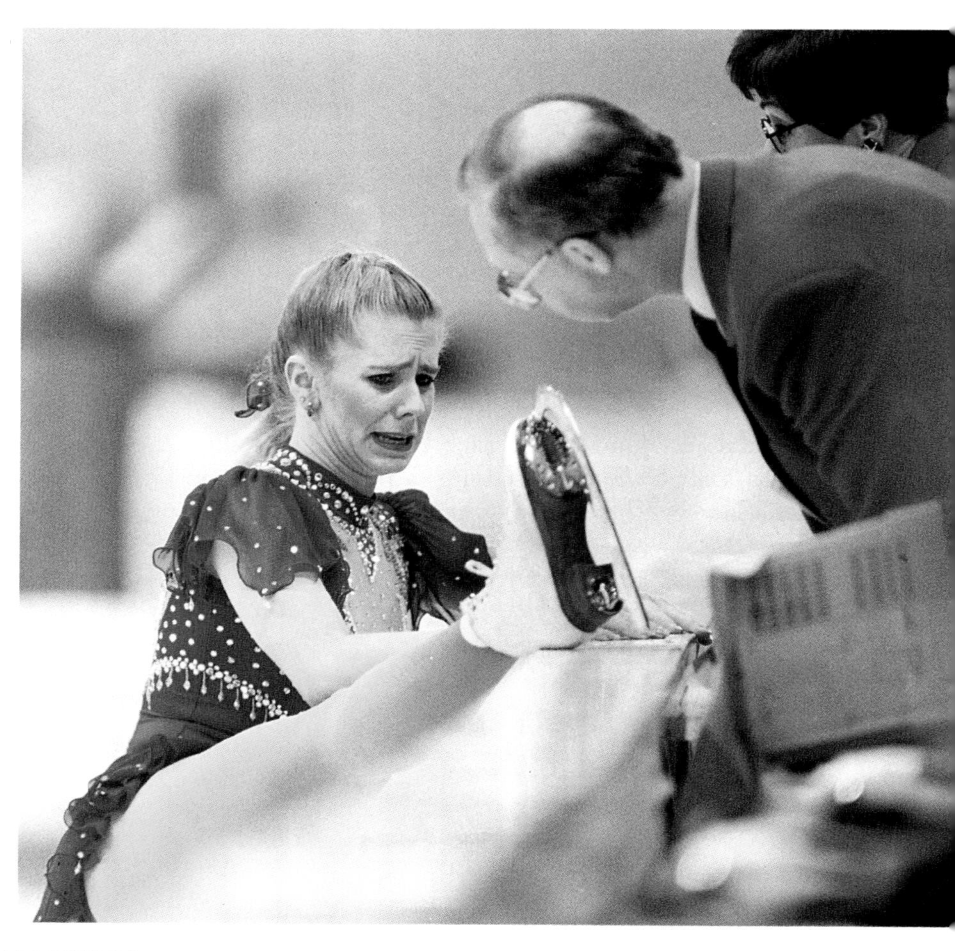

The Lillehammer judges allowed a tearful Tonya to replace a broken skate lace (right); but a nonplussed Nancy won the keys to the Magic Kingdom.

DEPP CHARGE

No one takes more risks than the Gielgud of grunge. He has played a freak with scissors for hands, a sleazy cross-dressing Hollywood director (*Ed Wood*) and a dysfunctional Buster Keaton (*Benny & Joon*). Offscreen, '94 seemed to be Johnny Depp's year of living *too* dangerously. The chain-smoking, tattoo-festooned, Viper Room-owning movie star acted out a hotel brawl with superwaif supermodel girlfriend Kate Moss that resulted in a trashed $1,200-per-night room and a handcuffed Depp, 31. He was arrested on charges of criminal mischief for his actions at New York City's tony Mark Hotel. Police suspected he was drunk and had been fighting with Moss, 20, for whom he left his former love, *Edward Scissorhands* costar Winona Ryder. After several hours in a holding cell, he was released and told that the charges would be dismissed if he stayed out of trouble for six months and agreed to reimburse the Mark $9,767.12 in damages and guest fees.

That was just the most highly publicized of Depp's recent problems. He had been arrested on three previous occasions: for getting into a tiff with an L.A. police officer over a jaywalking ticket, for speeding in Arizona and for assaulting a hotel security guard in Vancouver. To many of Depp's friends these incidents are just Johnny being Johnny. "I think Johnny obviously has a temper, but this is a minor incident," says John Waters, who directed Depp in *Cry-Baby*. "The room service must have been bad." Meantime, Depp is even having his WINONA FOREVER tattoo removed from his right bicep, a painful procedure that is done one letter at a time. At the time of his arrest it read WINO FOREVER.

A handcuffed Depp is escorted from a New York City police van after a hotel-trashing incident.

"He took everything away from me!" said Holly Ramona of her father, Gary (in the courtroom during her testimony).

A FATHER FIGHTS BACK

Gary Ramona, 50, was stunned in 1990 when his daughter, Holly, now 23, who was in treatment with psychotherapist Marche Isabella for bulimia, asked, "Why did you rape me?" Holly had, she said, belatedly remembered that her father had sexually abused her as a child. (Recovered memory—in which suppressed traumatic events can be brought to light—has become one of the most controversial areas of modern psychiatry, coming under attack for having the potential for quackery.)

After Holly's allegations, Ramona's wife, Stephanie, 49, filed for divorce. Gary, who vehemently denied the allegations, had no subsequent contact with her, Holly or his other daughters, Kelli, 22, and Shauna, 17. By 1991, Ramona had lost his job as a vice president at the Robert Mondavi Winery. In his view, blame for all this lay with therapist Isabella and her colleague, Dr. Richard Rose, who, Ramona maintains, planted the idea of abuse in his daughter's mind. "They destroyed my beautiful family," he says.

Ramona filed an $8 million malpractice suit, but at the civil trial in Napa, California, separating fact from fantasy was difficult. Gary depicted his daughter as enjoying a normal childhood; Holly demurred, telling the court her father often yelled at the children and was distant. In therapy for eating disorder and depression, Holly testified that she suffered flashbacks of her father abusing her. On the stand, her mother said she had harbored suspicions. "It was like putting together a puzzle," she said. "I would have given my life if the pieces didn't fit, but they did." Despite the testimony, the jury awarded Ramona a $500,000 settlement for lost wages. Now he faces a civil suit brought by Holly to recover money for her therapy, which she says was necessary because of his abuse. She remains certain about what happened. "In my heart," she says, "I'll always know the verdict."

Memories of abuse, Holly testified, "made me feel dirty and disgusting."

THE PRICE WASN'T RIGHT

"I never thought it would happen to me. I'm 70 years old. The sexual revolution in my life came when I was out of ammunition," laments Bob Barker. But deep into life's bonus round, he was under fire, accused of sexual harassment. The charges were leveled by Dian Parkinson, a model who worked with him on *The Price Is Right* for 18 years.

There was no disagreement over whether Barker, a widower since 1981 after 37 years of marriage, and the unmarried Parkinson, 49, had a physical relationship. The liaisons, by Barker's account, took place at his house, at her apartment and in his studio dressing room. At issue, rather, was whether Parkinson's job was at stake in her getting involved with Barker. Parkinson claimed that she had sex with her boss only because she feared losing her $120,000 annual salary. She asked for $8 million to settle out of court. Barker refused. "She is not telling the truth," he says. "I think it's an injustice to the women who really are suffering when a woman files a cynical lawsuit for personal gain." He says he broke off the relationship in 1991 to avoid possible problems in the shop, and she left in 1993.

Parkinson refused to talk about her charges, but Barker was open about their "fling." "She told me I had always been so straitlaced that it was time I had some hanky-panky in my life," he says. "She volunteered to provide the hanky-panky." Some of their coworkers on *Price* claim they knew what was going on. Recalls India Ditto, who retired as Barker's hairdresser in 1992: "I was afraid of cutting her fingers because she had her hands in his hair all the time."

"If anyone was doing the harassing on that set, it was Dian," says Janice Pennington (second from left). In 1988 she posed with Barker and fellow Price *models (from left) Dian Parkinson, Holly Hallstrom and Kathleen Bradley.*

"I'm starting to realize how valuable I am—that it could all go away much faster than it came," says Dre at home.

A Doctor in the Big House?

"We can *talk* about killing people, but everyone knows we ain't killed no motherf--kers ," says millionaire rapper and record producer Dr. Dre, 29. The Grammy-winning Dre's songs on the albums *The Chronic* and *Doggystyle* (produced for his protege Snoop Doggy Dogg) both earned platinum, despite, or perhaps because of, their controversial lyrics. Not only do they contain offensive language, they also glorify debauchery and getting high. The records of Dre, who changed his name from Andre Young in honor of basketball star Julius (Dr. J) Erving, have been denounced by many as misogynistic and by the Reverend Jesse Jackson, who has attacked rap's repeated use of the words "nigger" and "bitches." But, says Dre dismissively, "We take episodes that we've seen and been through and put them into songs."

He had an episode himself in '94 that deserved—and got—a rap, sending him to the slammer. No stranger to courtrooms, in 1992 he pleaded guilty to battery of a police officer during a brawl in New Orleans and served 30 days under house arrest. The following year he settled out of court with Denise Barnes, a former Fox TV talk show host who accused him of assaulting her in a nightclub. In '93, Dre pleaded no contest to breaking the jaw of a record producer during an argument and was again sentenced to house arrest.

This year, he pleaded no contest to drunk driving charges after leading police on a chase through Beverly Hills in his Ferrari at speeds up to 90 m.p.h. The judge ruled that the conviction violated his parole agreement in the battery case and sentenced him to eight months in jail and attendance at an alcohol education program. "I've made some f--kups," says Dre, "but I've paid for them." Still, that doesn't mean he'll stop carrying a gun. "It's defense," says Dre. "If everybody on the street has one and you don't, you automatically lose the chess match. Checkmate. I'd rather be judged by 12 than carried by six."

LAWYERS MUST LEARN

The war is far from over, but the opening battle was decisively won when former legal secretary Rena Weeks triumphed in a record-book sexual harassment case in San Francisco. Though she won't see a penny until the end of an appeals process that could go all the way to the Supreme Court, Weeks, 40, was first awarded $7.1 million in punitive damages—believed to be the largest such award ever—in a suit against the prestigious law firm of Baker & McKenzie and former partner Martin R. Greenstein, 49. (The amount was later reduced to $3.5 million, which Weeks may appeal.)

During the five-week trial, Weeks and half a dozen other female former employees told of the lewd remarks and gropings that they said Greenstein had subjected them to as far back as 1988. Weeks, who held a $35,000-a-year job at Baker & McKenzie for three months in 1991, testified that on one occasion Greenstein, a divorced father of four, grabbed her breast while dropping M&Ms into the pocket of her blouse. Then "he put his knee in my lower back and pulled me back . . . and he said, 'Let's see which breast is bigger.' I was in shock."

Greenstein vigorously denied the allegations, claiming Weeks was not a victim but an incompetent and disgruntled employee. (After Weeks complained about Greenstein to her superiors, he was sent to counseling and was eventually asked to resign.) For their part, jurors were not persuaded that Baker & McKenzie did its best to prevent such behavior. Notes juror William Carpenter: "I got the feeling of power, arrogance and outright lies. If there's one message I'd like to send out, it's that even attorneys aren't above the law."

Greenstein (above left), with his lawyer, argued that he was himself a victim of changing standards in the workplace; Weeks, with her attorneys, exulted at the decision. "As a worker, as a secretary . . . we don't have to get stepped on."

SAVIORS & SURVIVORS

Caught in the extremes that test us most— war and revolution, **FLOOD** *and* **FIRE**—*some excelled, some endured*

TWO AMERICAN PROFILES IN COURAGE

It began as a gentle drizzle, but by the time the downpour ended in eastern Texas, it had become a deluge of almost Biblical proportions. Tropical storm Rosa had dumped more than 20 inches of rain on the area in 36 hours, flooding 26 counties and forcing more than 10,000 people from their homes.

Tannie Shannon, 49, and his wife Frances, 51, were at home in Forest Hills, 35 miles outside Houston, babysitting for their 11-month-old granddaughter Andrea, when the rains came. "First there was just a little water," says Shannon, a local video distributor. "Next thing, we couldn't drive out through it. All of a sudden it was coming in the house, and we decided to walk on out."

Half walk, half swim was more like it. To protect Andrea from the neck-deep water, the Shannons swathed her in plastic bunting to keep her dry. They put a leash on the family's Old English sheepdog and forged down the street to a neighbor's truck. Their struggle was captured by *Dallas Morning News* photographer David Leeson, and his dramatic picture (left) made front pages across the country. "It wouldn't be fair to say we weren't scared," says Tannie Shannon. "But we were mostly afraid for our granddaughter." Andrea was a trouper. "She got a little wet, but she was happy as a lark," says Shannon. "She wasn't upset at all." Nor were her grandparents overwhelmed. "It'll be a couple of days before the water goes down," noted Shannon calmly. "And then I guess we'll go back and start cleaning up the mess."

The Texas flood was "real nasty," says Tannie Shannon (above left), who sought safety with granddaughter Andrea, wife Frances and sheepdog Amadeus. In Idaho's Boise National Forest, a fire fighter battling the summer's devastation checks his progress.

Representative of the thousands of forest firefighters—both professional and volunteer—who heroically battled the infernos that raged last summer through the Western states was the elite 20-member Hot Shot team, specialists in tackling major blazes, from little Prineville, Oregon. Called in to assist on a fire on Colorado's Storm King Mountain, about five miles outside the resort town of Glenwood Springs, the Hot Shots battled what was still a relatively modest blaze. Then, in a matter of seconds, the wind changed direction and intensified; almost instantly the crews were trapped in an inferno. "Being on the ridge was like standing on the surface of the sun and trying to run someplace cool," says Hot Shot Tom Rambo, 22. "I don't know if there's such a thing as an organized panic, but that's what it was. We stuck together like we always do."

Still, when the blowup, as firefighters call it, was over, 14, including four women, had been killed in one of the worst disasters ever to befall American forest firefighters. Among the dead were nine members of the Prineville Hot Shots. Traumatized by the experience, the survivors tried to come to terms with the horror and heroism they saw there. A mass memorial service was held in Prineville, and Rambo spoke for many when he said, "I don't think I'd cried in 10 years, but I cried for two days. We knew every one of those people, and we loved them."

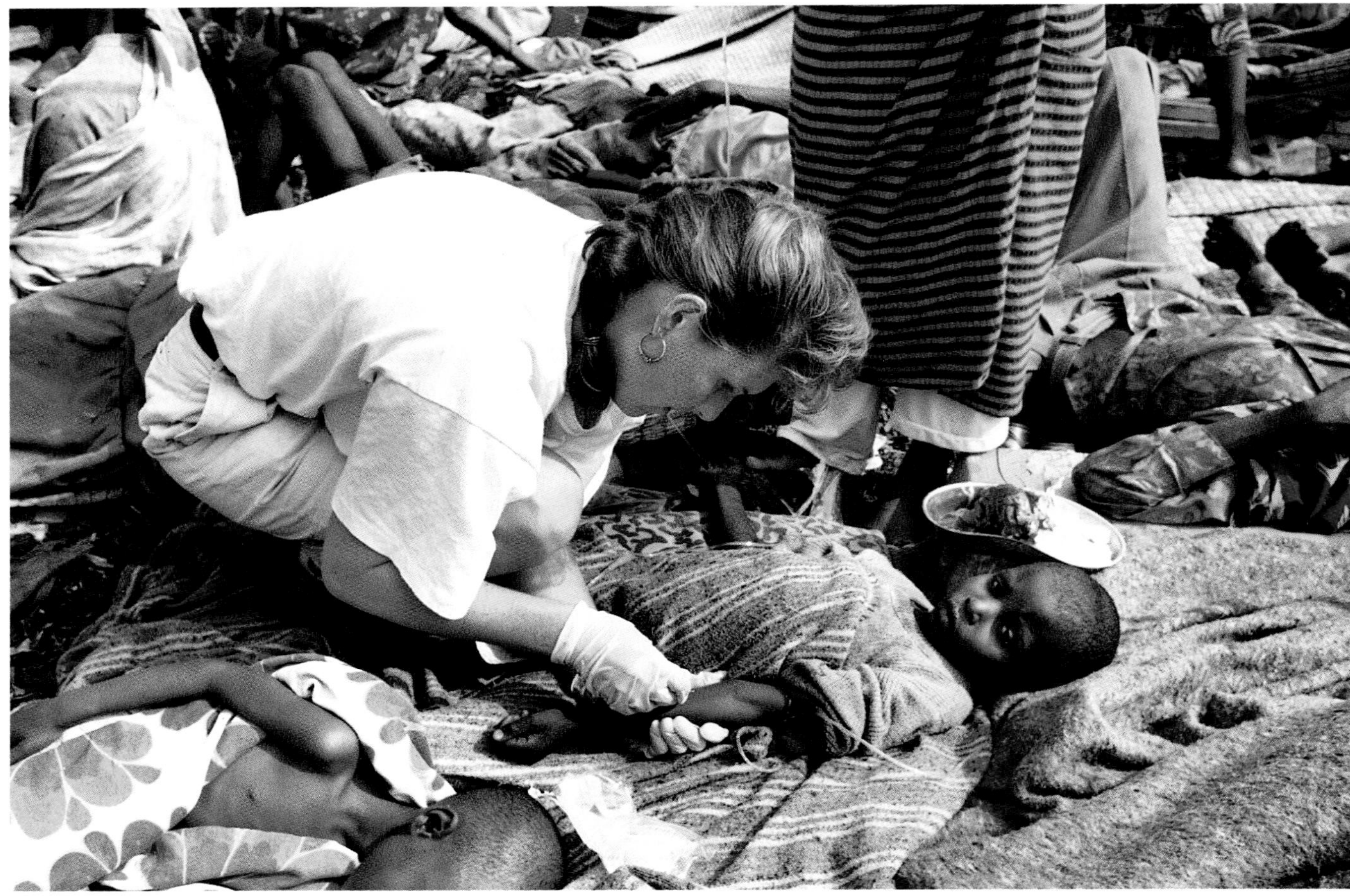

"It's very difficult," says Kasprow of fighting cholera in Rwanda. "Every day the numbers increase."

FIGHTING FOR LIFE

On the outskirts of Goma, Zaire, where a million Rwandans—one-eighth of their country's population—fled from a genocidal civil war, refugees died by the thousands from cholera and dysentery, thirst and starvation. With few words and little evident emotion, Jody Kasprow, 26, begins her morning rounds at a primitive field hospital. For the next three hours, the nurse from Vancouver, British Columbia, will separate the living from the dead, equipped with little but her own courage. She was one of about 25 relief workers deployed by CONCERN Worldwide, a relief organization based in Dublin.

Bending over a woman, she slaps her on the leg. Seeing no movement, she throws the woman's wrap over her head. Today more than 250 bodies will be taken to mass graves. "It's upsetting," says Kasprow, as she wipes her brow, careful not to touch her face with gloved hands that have been immersed in the muck of cholera victims. "The weak, the old and the very young are probably going to die. That's difficult to accept, but it's a fact. You get a bit numb."

In the evening, when she returns to a house that the organization Doctors Without Borders has rented, she eats her one daily meal: potatoes, tomatoes and onions. Foreigners—even Kasprow, who receives about $20 a week for expenses—can afford to eat. "But carrying dead bodies doesn't lead to a healthy appetite," she says.

A long, strange trip brought Kasprow to Africa. In 1992 she went on a safari and fell in love with both the continent and her tour guide. She saved her money and moved to Johannesburg the following year. The relationship with the guide ended, but her commitment to Africa did not, and she quickly found work with CONCERN. Kasprow labored on famine relief in Mozambique and Angola, often improvising medical care. Says her friend Patty Hansinger: "Jody never subscribed to the materialism of our society. She was looking for more of a challenge. She found it in Africa."

DIARY OF DESPAIR

"Today a shell fell on the park in front of my house," reads a 1992 entry. "A lot of people were hurt. AND NINA IS DEAD . . . We went to kindergarten together . . . I cry and wonder why." With her childhood stolen by the carnage in Sarajevo, 13-year-old Zlata Filipović kept a journal that gave a fresh and rending voice to Bosnia's tragedy. Much like Anne Frank, who wrote her famous diary while hiding from Nazi troops in World War II, Zlata addressed her writing to an imaginary friend. Starting at age 10, the A student who had a passion for pizza, MTV and Michael Jackson recorded her despair, her small consolations and the war's impact on her family and friends. The resulting eloquent chronicle was eventually published as *Zlata's Diary: A Child's Life in Sarajevo*, and became a world-wide success, with editions in 36 countries. It sold 200,000 copies in the U.S., and a film of it is in development.

The only child of a middle-class couple of Muslim, Croat and Serb descent, Zlata, now 14, was flown out to Paris with her father Malik, a lawyer, and her mother Alica, a biochemist, by French authorities. The family, which is slowly healing from the traumas of war, settled there in exile, following the whirlwind of publicity for Zlata's book. Serious, poised and troubled by the fate of her country, Zlata, says a spokeswoman for her French publisher, "still doesn't have the heart for activities like Girl Scouts. All her spare time is devoted to Sarajevo, writing letters, getting news, sending packages." And waiting for peace. Says Zlata: "I hope soon we can go back to Sarajevo. I have to hope. It's just hope that keeps me going on."

Zlata (in Sarajevo in 1993) says, "My heart wants to go back, but it's crazy. I have to stay away until it's over."

HOPE IN HAITI

Among the powerful personalities who focused their concern, care and diplomatic expertise on the confusing, crippling situation in Haiti, none was more galvanizing than Randall Robinson, 52. The respected civil rights leader and lobbyist—praised for his activism in getting Congress to adopt sanctions against South Africa in the '80s—dramatized the cause with a life-threatening hunger strike. He vowed to eat nothing until the Clinton Administration changed its policy of turning away Haitian refugees from U.S. shores. After 27 days, thanks in part to media coverage and support from Jesse Jackson and many Congress members, Anthony Lake, the President's National Security Advisor, informed Robinson that the White House was changing course. Robinson was gratified but wary. "This is just an intermediate result," he said. "Tomorrow is another day."

Another unlikely figure picked up the ball. With invasion troops on the way to Haiti, Jimmy Carter, 70, ex-President and canny freelance diplomat fresh from negotiating a nuclear freeze in North Korea, sat in Port-au-Prince with Haitian army leader Lt. Gen. Raoul Cédras and hammered out a deal to peacefully restore power to ousted President Jean-Bertrand Aristide. That ended the reign of bloodshed and political terror that had gripped the island country since 1991. The deal, without doubt, saved many lives which would have been lost in an armed invasion.

Fourteen years after he was routed from office—scorned as an ineffectual and often naive leader by fellow Democrats—Carter proved once again that there are second acts in American politics. The man from Plains, Georgia, had to fight for his Haitian victory, though. Secretary of State Warren Christopher, among others, was opposed to deputizing Carter for the mission. And Carter balked when he found that his instructions left him little room for negotiating with Cédras. He demanded, and got, more flexibility. On his return, Carter was whisked off by an escort to spend the night in the Lincoln bedroom at the White House, a guest of the current resident. His first amused thought: "They're trying to keep me away from CNN!" Reluctant to let others, even the President, do his talking for him, Carter said, "I got up at 6:30 and called CNN myself."

Events lurched on for a bloody and bedraggled Haiti (clockwise from top left): Randall Robinson prays and fasts; Jimmy Carter (followed by ex-Joint Chiefs Chairman Colin Powell and Georgia Senator Sam Nunn) arrives in Haiti; a reinstated President Aristide releases a dove of peace; and General Raul Cédras and his family head off for asylum in Panama.

THE LADY IS A BULLDOG

Shannon Faulkner, 19, knows a thing or two about combat. For two years the South Carolinian has waged an unrelenting legal campaign against sex discrimination to become the first female corps member at the Citadel, Charleston's venerable military college. With the encouragement of her businessman father Ed and mother Sandy, a schoolteacher, she applied. The Citadel originally offered her entrance, unaware of her gender and not having asked. They later rescinded when her sex was discovered. While awaiting a ruling on the latest appeal in the case (which may eventually go to the Supreme Court), Faulkner attends classes under court order as a day student. "It's becoming inevitable that I'm going to win," she declares. "They're just going to have to live with it."

Though the last legal stay spared her from the school's "knob" buzzcut, she has endured everything from death threats to hissing from cadets when she spoke in class. Her parents' home has been vandalized a number of times. Faulkner says she had "no idea what I was getting into"—but wouldn't dream of backing down. "I believe in it too much." Fortunately there have been a few brighter spots for the sophomore, whose goal is to become a teacher. (She remains undecided about a military career.)

Shannon's brave stance has attracted a number of admirers, including Citadel alum Pat Conroy, whose novel *Lords of Discipline* took an unflattering look at the college's hazing culture. "Shannon Faulkner is the bravest person who ever walked through Lesesne Gate at the Citadel," says Conroy. "She has stood alone facing the 2,000-man corps and has not blinked."

"I've learned that family is the most important thing," says Faulkner (in Charleston), "because they've been so supportive."

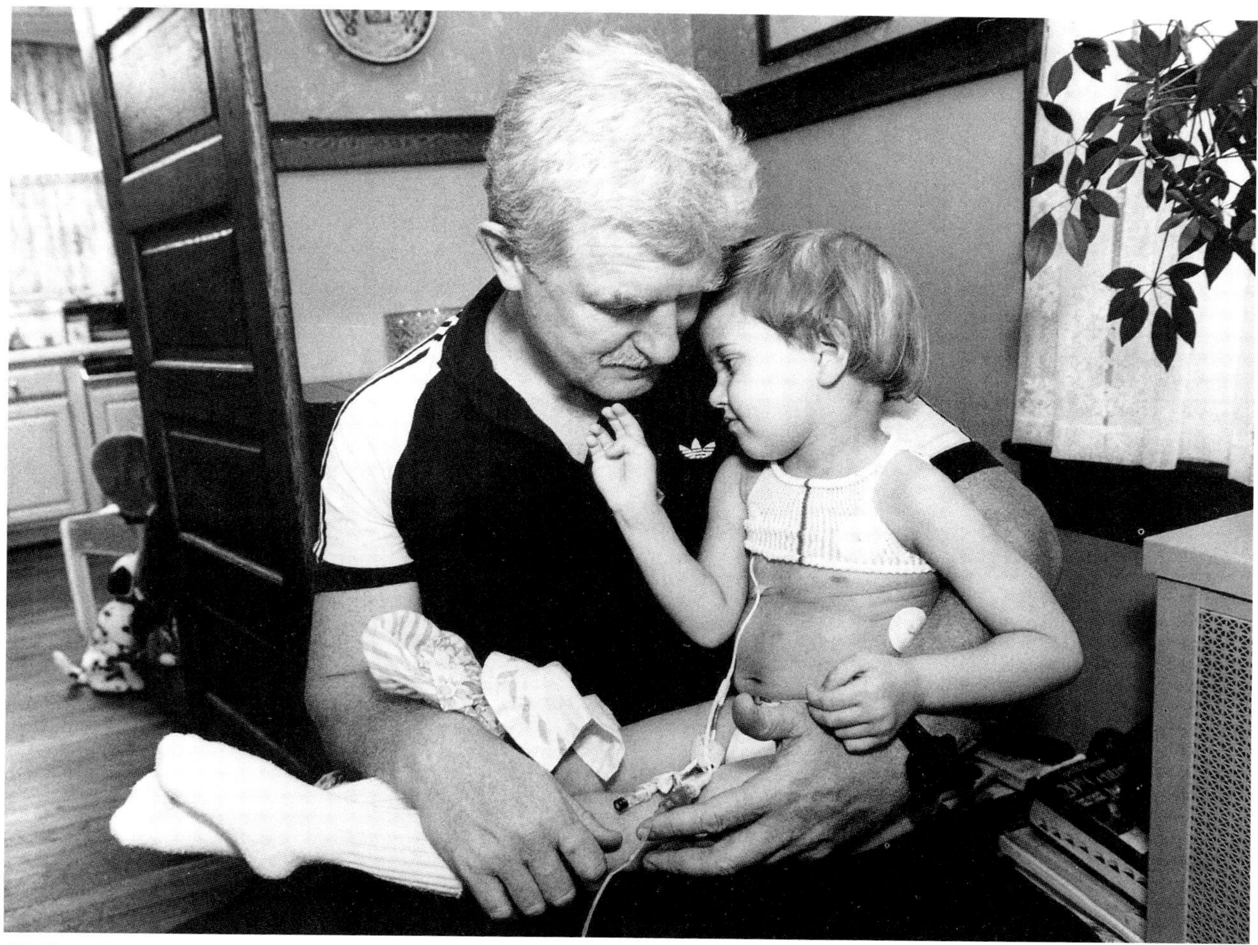

"Politics has driven my life for 15 years," says Moran (holding Dorothy). "Now it seems so secondary in importance."

MOMENT OF CRISIS

On health care, Representative Jim Moran (D-Va.) staked out a cautiously centrist position on reform. He was well insured by the Congressional health plan and dubious about the call for universal coverage. Why, he asked, should the government force employers to provide health care for their workers? The answer hit home in August when Jim, 49, and his wife, Mary, 38, learned that their second child, Dorothy, 3, was suffering from medulloblastoma, a deadly form of brain cancer. Doctors removed the peach-sized tumor but found the cancer had spread to her spine. Despite a painful course of chemotherapy, her prognosis remains dim: Doctors give her only a 30 percent chance of survival past age 5.

Understandably the diagnosis has devastated Moran, a gregarious, Boston-reared stockbroker, who was first elected to political office in 1979. "Everything was turned upside down," he says. "From that moment on, our lives have never been the same." When the previously divorced Moran wed Mary Mallet in 1988, he resolved to balance work and family in his second marriage. He made time for Dorothy and her brother Patrick, 5, a priority. And suddenly, in a tough re-election battle, Moran found himself in the position of millions of wage earners whose health care is tied to employment. He did win in November, and re-vowed to take up the fight for universal coverage of children. "It's unfair for innocent kids to suffer because their parents can't afford to pay," he says. Personally, Moran says, "I've been changed a lot by Dorothy's cancer. I've learned that you have to enjoy your kids when they're healthy and happy. Spend time with them. All the nice words and toys in the world can't make up for not spending time. I used to think the last five years of my life were heaven. Now my idea of heaven is totally different. Heaven will be seeing Dorothy recover."

Some lustrous celebs collected the year's glittering prizes, and joined **STEVEN SPIELBERG**'*s ultimate power table; others, like ex-Colonel Ollie North, were left in the dust*

WINNERS & LOSERS

Cheers! Bruce Springsteen, Tom Hanks and Steven Spielberg celebrated their Oscar triumphs at Elton John's AIDS benefit at the Beverly Hills restaurant Maple Drive. Joining the late-night toasts were, from left, Spielberg's wife Kate Capshaw, Elton, Bruce, wife Patti Scialfa, Hanks's sister-in-law Lily Reeves, Tom, his wife Rita Wilson and Steven. It doesn't get heavier than this, folks.

66TH ANNUAL OSCAR AWARDS
(Presented March 21, 1994)
Picture: *Schindler's List*
Actor: Tom Hanks, *Philadelphia*
Actress: Holly Hunter, *The Piano*
Supporting Actor: Tommy Lee Jones, *The Fugitive*
Supporting Actress: Anna Paquin, *The Piano*
Director: Steven Spielberg, *Schindler's List*
Original Screenplay: Jane Campion, *The Piano*
Adapted Screenplay: Steven Zaillian, *Schindler's List*
Music, Original Song: "Streets of Philadelphia," by Bruce Springsteen, from *Philadelphia*
Jean Hersholt Award: Paul Newman for humanitarian efforts
Honorary Award: Deborah Kerr for career achievement

ANNA PAQUIN

What a cloche call! For her role in *The Piano*, 11-year-old Anna Paquin scooped the Best Supporting Actress Oscar from under the noses of such high-powered rivals as Winona Ryder (*The Age of Innocence*), Emma Thompson (*In the Name of the Father*) and Holly Hunter (*The Firm*). Paquin, who had yet to see her own film because of its adult rating in her native New Zealand, also won Most Surprising Headgear for her beguiling beaded snood.

TIM ALLEN

Memo to *Home Improvement* executives:

Let's not point fingers, but one of you screwups forgot to nominate our 41-year-old ABC star, Tim Allen, for an Emmy. We had TV's top-rated show, so Tim would have been a shoo-in. As you can see by his enclosed picture, he is not happy about our oversight.

DENNIS FRANZ

So he doesn't wear a weave. And his profile won't stop traffic. And his hot-and-handsome *NYPD Blue* partner David Caruso walked out on him, leaving him to portray the dyspeptic, alcoholic, profane detective Andy Sipowicz with replacement Jimmy Smits. So much the better. Because when the Emmy for Best Actor in a Drama Series was announced, Dennis Franz (posing above with a duet of models), who has, by his own count, portrayed 28 cops on screens big and small, gleefully picked up the statuette.

The son of German immigrants was probably born to play a man in blue. At his suburban Chicago high school, Franz was nicknamed the Peacekeeper for mediating altercations between rival cliques. When filming *Blue* on location in New York City, members of the *real* NYPD flock admiringly around him. "I can relate to police officers," says Franz. "I find them to be pretty insightful." Still, when he heads for his antique-filled home in Bel Air, the actor leaves the gun and the cuffs in the prop room. And a good thing, too. Joanie Zeck, 46, Franz's live-in girlfriend for a decade, frowns on squad-room machismo. At his 50th birthday party in October, Franz, who helped Zeck raise her two daughters from a previous marriage, finally popped the question. "Unlike Sipowitz, Dennis doesn't swear, ever," says the future Mrs. Franz. And with very good reason. "When I spout dirty words on TV, she gives me a slug on the arm," marvels Franz. "God forbid I should ever have to drop my pants!"

46TH ANNUAL EMMY AWARDS
(Presented Sept. 12, 1994)
Drama Series: *Picket Fences*
Comedy Series: *Frasier*
Variety, Music or Comedy Series: *Late Show With David Letterman*
Miniseries: *Prime Suspect 3*
Lead Actor, Drama Series: Dennis Franz, *NYPD Blue*
Lead Actress, Drama Series: Sela Ward, *Sisters*
Lead Actor, Comedy Series: Kelsey Grammer, *Frasier*
Lead Actress, Comedy Series: Candice Bergen, *Murphy Brown*
Lead Actor, Miniseries or Special: Hume Cronyn, *To Dance With the White Dog*
Lead Actress, Miniseries or Special: Kirstie Alley, *David's Mother*
Supporting Actor, Drama Series: Fyvush Finkel, *Picket Fences*
Supporting Actress, Drama Series: Leigh Taylor-Young, *Picket Fences*
Supporting Actor, Comedy Series: Michael Richards, *Seinfeld*
Supporting Actress, Comedy Series: Laurie Metcalf, *Roseanne*
Supporting Actor, Miniseries or Special: Michael Goorjian, *David's Mother*
Supporting Actress, Miniseries or Special: Cicely Tyson, *The Oldest Confederate Widow Tells All*
Individual Performance, Variety or Music Program: Tracey Ullman, *Tracey Ullman: Takes on New York*

21ST ANNUAL DAYTIME EMMY AWARDS
(Presented May 25, 1994)
Drama: *All My Children*
Talk Show: *The Oprah Winfrey Show*
Game Show: *Jeopardy!*
Actress: Hillary B. Smith, *One Life to Live*
Actor: Michael Zaslow, *Guiding Light*
Supporting Actress: Susan Haskell, *One Life to Live*
Supporting Actor: Justin Deas, *Guiding Light*
Talk Show Host: Oprah Winfrey

MICHAEL ZASLOW

Maybe Michael Zaslow, 51, could have won a Daytime Emmy for longevity instead of Best Actor. He has been *Guiding Light*'s mean-minded Roger Thorpe for some 20 years. He and wife Susan Hufford, a psychotherapist, have two adopted Korean-born daughters.

SUSAN HASKELL

On *One Life to Live*, Toronto's Susan Haskell plays against type as Marty Saybrook, survivor of a troubled childhood and sexual assault. After she won the Daytime Emmy, the Manhattan apartment she shares with sister Carolyn, a model, "looked like a flower shop," says Haskell.

Salt 'n Pepa & En Vogue

For the spiciest chic of '94, rappers Salt 'n Pepa mixed it up with popsters En Vogue for joint honors. From left: EV's Maxine Jones, S&P's Dede Roper, EV's Terry Ellis, S&P's Sandy Denton, EV's Dawn Robinson, S&P's Cheryl James and EV's Cindy Herron.

MTV VIDEO MUSIC AWARDS
(Presented Sept. 8, 1994)
Best Video: Aerosmith, "Cryin'"
Male: Tom Petty and the Heartbreakers, "Mary Jane's Last Dance"
Female: Janet Jackson, "If"
Group: Aerosmith, "Cryin'"
Rap: Snoop Doggy Dogg, "Doggy Dogg World"
Dance: Salt 'n Pepa with En Vogue, "Whatta Man"
Metal/Hard rock: Soundgarten, "Black Hole Sun"
Alternative: Nirvana, "Heart-Shaped Box"
New Artist: Counting Crows, *Mr. Jones*
R&B: Salt 'n Pepa with En Vogue, "Whatta Man"
Direction: R.E.M., "Everybody Hurts" (Jake Scott, director)

Snoop Doggy Dogg

In every sense, the Dogg (a.k.a. Calvin Broadus), 22, had his day in '94. He picked up an MTV Award for his languid gangsta rapping while still awaiting trial in L.A. on charges of being an accessory to murder.

36TH ANNUAL GRAMMY AWARDS

(Presented March 1, 1994)

Record of the Year: "I Will Always Love You," Whitney Houston

Song of the Year: "A Whole New World (Aladdin's Theme)," Alan Menken and Tim Rice

Album of the Year: *The Bodyguard*, Whitney Houston

New Artist: Toni Braxton

Male Pop Vocal: "If I Ever Lose My Faith in You," Sting

Female Pop Vocal: "I Will Always Love You," Whitney Houston

Pop Vocal by a Duo or Group: "A Whole New World (Aladdin's Theme)," Peabo Bryson and Regina Belle

Traditional Pop Performance: "Steppin' Out," Tony Bennett

Rock Song: "Runaway Train," David Pirner

Solo Rock Vocal: "I'd Do Anything for Love (But I Won't Do That)," Meat Loaf

Rock Vocal by a Duo or Group: "Livin' on the Edge," Aerosmith

R&B Song: "That's the Way Love Goes," Janet Jackson, James Harris III and Terry Lewis

Male R&B Vocal: "A Song for You," Ray Charles

Female R&B Vocal: "Another Sad Love Song," Toni Braxton

R&B Vocal by a Duo or Group: "No Ordinary Love," Sade

Rap Solo: "Let Me Ride," Dr. Dre

Rap Performance by a Duo or Group: "Rebirth of Slick," Digable Planets

Hard Rock Performance: "Plush," Stone Temple Pilots

Metal Performance: "I Don't Want to Change the World," Ozzy Osbourne

Alternative Music Album: *Zooropa*, U2

MEAT LOAF

What? Meat Loaf again? Actually, the stolid rocker, now 46, always has something on his plate. His 1977 *Bat Out of Hell* remains the No. 2-selling album in history; his last effort, *Bat Out of Hell II*, sold 11 million copies, and its single hit, "I'd Do Anything for Love (But I Won't Do That)," earned him a tasty Grammy.

WHITNEY HOUSTON

For Pop's reigning diva, the '90s have been a split decision. Her film *The Bodyguard* grossed $300 million. In '94, she picked up 11 *Billboard* Music Awards, three Grammys, seven American Music Awards and the NAACP's Entertainer of the Year prize. She also did a live HBO concert from South Africa in November. But as the accolades piled up, so did the tabloid rumors: a relationship with model Cindy Crawford, troubles with hubby Bobby Brown, 26, and neglect of 18-month-old daughter Bobbi Kristina. Houston, 31, vehemently denied all the whispers.

28TH ANNUAL COUNTRY MUSIC AWARDS
(Presented Oct. 5, 1994)
Entertainer of the Year: Vince Gill
Male Vocalist: Vince Gill
Female Vocalist: Pam Tillis
Single: "I Swear," John Michael Montgomery
Album: *Common Thread: The Songs of the Eagles*, John Anderson, Clint Black, Suzy Bogguss, Brooks & Dunn, Billy Dean, Diamond Rio, Vince Gill, Alan Jackson, Little Texas, Lorrie Morgan, Travis Tritt, Tanya Tucker and Trisha Yearwood
Vocal Group: Diamond Rio
Duo: Brooks & Dunn
Music Video: "Independence Day," Martina McBride
Horizon Award: John Michael Montgomery
Song: "Chattahoochee," Alan Jackson-Jim McBride Vocal
Event: Reba McEntire with Linda Davis, "Does He Love You"
Musician: Mark O'Connor, fiddle

VINCE GILL

The performer with the heart-tugging tenor and the aw-shucks manner was 1994's hero of the hayloft. He didn't need a big hat or chiseled features to pull it off, either. As Oklahoma-born Vince Gill, 37, puts it, "I'm not a heartthrob type. I'm more Tom Hanks than Tom Cruise." Perhaps, but he not only hosted the Country Music Association Awards in October, he also took home three of them, including Male Vocalist of the Year, for an unprecedented fourth year in a row.

But at his spread on a private golf course in Franklin, Tennessee, outside Nashville, the low-key singer might need his father Stan Gill, a U.S. administrative law judge in Columbus, Ohio, to settle the genial family disputes over who sings loudest, longest and best. Although Gill broke through with "When I Call Your Name" in 1990, Janis, 40, his wife of 14 years, was the first to lasso a hit. In the '80s, she and sister Kristine Arnold, as the Sweethearts of the Rodeo duo, had seven Top 10 country tunes. And now their daughter Jenny, 12, is hinting she'd like to record. (She sang a track with dad on his '93 Christmas album *Let There Be Peace on Earth*.) As a trio in the making, the Gills have perfected one odd anthem arrangement. As part of their Thanksgiving ritual, Janis beats time on the turkey before it goes into the oven while Vince strums a tune on the guitar and Jenny toots harmony on her flute. The Gills even phone relatives and serenade them with "The Turkey Slap." Do we smell another hit?

Tommy Moe

"I am in a zone right now where I almost can't stop myself from skiing fast," said the unsung Alaskan, as he became the first American since 1984 to garner Alpine gold. The win was the sweeter because Moe, 24, a fiercely focused competitor, had been kicked off the U.S. ski team at age 16 for drinking and smoking marijuana.

Bonnie Blair

Five, count 'em, five gold medals (the last two in Lillehammer) have made Milwaukee's unassuming Bonnie Blair, 28, America's most gilded woman Olympian—surpassing sprinter Evelyn Ashford, swimmer Janet Evans and diver Pat McCormick, who have four each. The peppy speed skater, who is now the indefatigable spokesperson of Skippy peanut butter, didn't resort to visualizations or sports psychologists to improve her phenomenal performance. Her philosophy: "You can't count on winning, so you have to make it happen."

DAN JANSEN

After failing in two previous Winter Games, Dan Jansen, 28, finally struck gold. Dubbed "skating's nicest human," the Wisconsin native scooped up his year-old baby Jane (named after his sister, who died of leukemia in 1988) and skated Lillehammer's sweetest victory lap.

U.S. GOLD MEDALISTS, THE WINTER OLYMPICS
Lillehammer, Norway (February 12-27, 1994)
Men's Skiing: Tommy Moe, *downhill*
Men's Skating: Dan Jansen, *1,000-meter speed skating*
Women's Skiing: Diann Roffe-Steinrotter, *super giant slalom*
Women's Skating: Cathy Turner, *500-meter short-track speed skating;* Bonnie Blair, *1,000-meter speed skating and 500-meter speed skating*

DAVE'S MOM

Amid the gusty commentators and fur-trimmed anchor types, Dave Letterman's mom, Dorothy, with her folksy *Late Show* reports, was TV's Norway star. The ageless (it's a secret) cottontop even scooped the pack with an interview of Hillary Clinton. "Can you do anything about the speed limit in Connecticut?" she asked on behalf of her son, who lived (and sped) there.

FIELD OF SCHEMES

Bang the drum slowly. And roll out the infield covers. In '94 baseball struck out, and it was the fans who had to hit the showers: Season canceled, playoffs nixed and, for the first time in 90 years, no World Series. At the bargaining table, owners demanded salary caps or a tax on payrolls to quell the enormous cost of fielding a dream; the players held firm in wanting a free market economy to determine their soaring value. So we turned to documentaries on PBS, or watched ex-hoopsters try Double-A ball, or even tuned in to Japanese baseball. Sadly, amid all the attention, our national pastime seemed past its time.

Some of it was corny, but the TV epic, Baseball, *by Ken Burns (above), 41, hit a homer. Exchanging three NBA title rings for a mitt in the minors, Michael Jordan (left), 31, showed that his glove work was not above the rim, and Oakland fans mugged before the meltdown.*

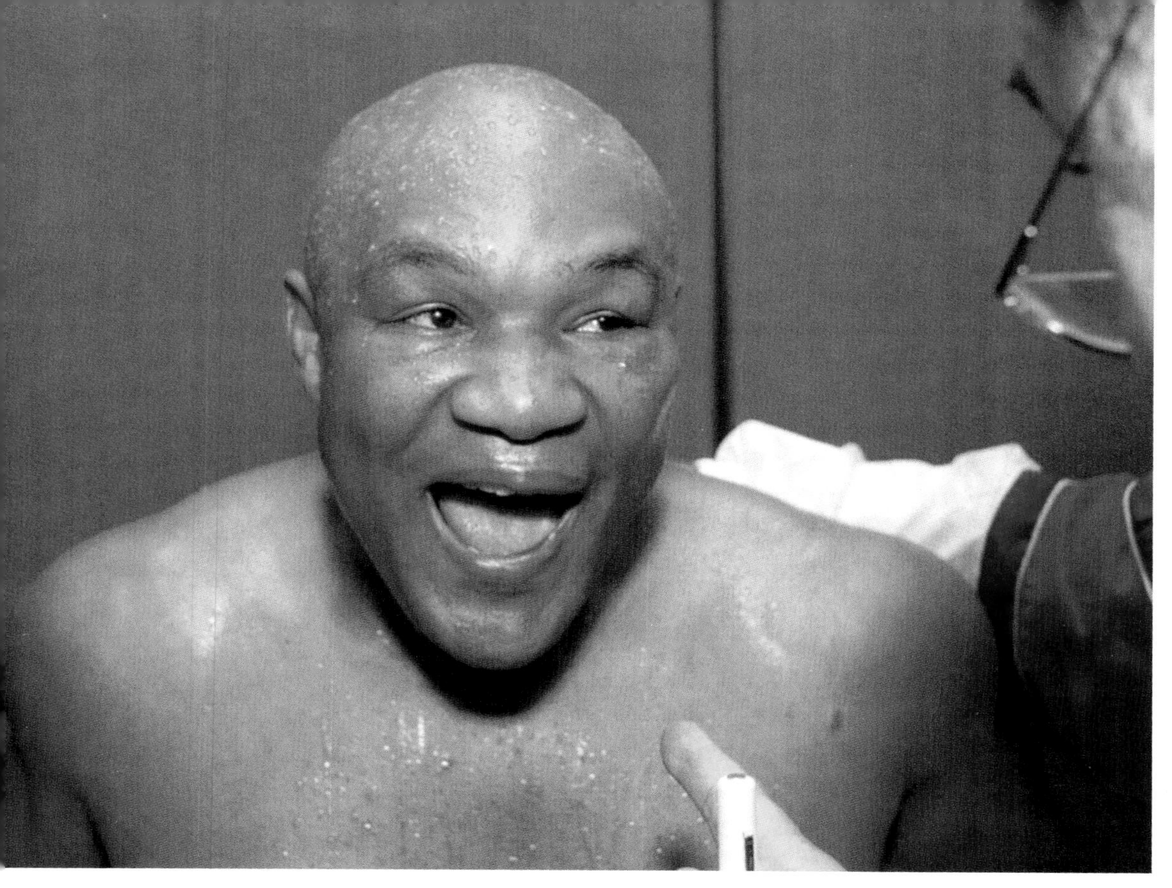

Elsewhere, happy surprise reigned. At 45, when most fighters are greeting the high rollers at Vegas casinos or making infomercials for vitamins, George Foreman (above) regained the heavyweight title he lost to Muhammad Ali in 1974. The win prompted Ali, 52, to quip, "Tell George I'm coming back." Meanwhile tennis's version of a grunge rocker, Andre Agassi, 24, released his liplock on Brooke Shields long enough to plant one on his first U.S. Open trophy.

INTERESTING WINNERS

Newt Gingrich, 51, mercury-tongued, eight-term Republican Congressman from Georgia and the incoming Speaker of the House.

Fred Thompson, 52, new Republican Senator from Tennessee, a minority counsel to the Senate Watergate Committee turned actor (*In the Line of Fire*, *Die Hard 2*).

Olympia Snowe, 47, new U.S. Senator from Maine after 16 years in the House, making her the eighth woman in the Senate (women will hold 47 of the 435 seats in the House).

WINNING KENNEDYS

Ted Kennedy, 62, the greatest legislator of the Kennedy brothers, taking his sixth and closest Senate election against another heir, Mitt Romney, 47, son of a former Michigan governor.

Patrick Kennedy, 27, the Senator's youngest child and a new U.S. Congressman from Rhode Island.

Joseph Kennedy II, 42, son of Robert and winner (unopposed) of a fifth term as Congressman from Massachusetts.

Kathleen Kennedy Townsend, 43, Bobby's daughter and new Maryland Lieutenant Governor.

Mark Kennedy Shriver, 30, son of former Peace Corps director Sargent Shriver, brother-in-law of Arnold Schwarzenegger and new member of the Maryland House of Delegates.

THEY'VE GOT YOU, BABE

In a shamelessly expensive and ugly election campaign, the Republicans capitalized on growing dissatisfaction with the societal pickle and with Bill Clinton to take control of Congress for the first time since the Eisenhower era. The anti-Democratic groundswell hit numerous statehouses as well. George W. Bush, 48, son of the former President, unhorsed Texas governor Ann Richards, despite shooting himself in the foot early in the race. On a photo-op dove-hunting trip (above) in a year of guns 'n poses, the Connecticut-born Bush brought down an endangered killdeer instead of a game bird.

Not all those embracing elephants gained office, though. Bush's brother Jeb, 41, lost the Florida governor's race, and Iran-Contra icon Oliver North (right), 51, lost to incumbent Senator Charles Robb, 55, who suffered from allegations of marital infidelity. Those who lie to Congress, apparently, do not fare as well as those who might have lied to their wives.

"The last thing I thought I would be is a U.S. Congressman, given all the bobcat vests and Eskimo boots I used to wear," said California Republican Sonny Bono (left, with wife Mary, 33). But that's just what happened to the 59-year-old former mayor of Palm Springs. Ex-wife Cher was less surprised. "I have no belief in the system," she told the New York Post, *"so Sonny's perfectly at home there. Politicians are one step below used-car salesmen."*

Back from prison (on a drug conviction) and rehab, Democrat Marion Barry (right), 58, reclaimed the Washington, D.C., mayoralty that he lost in 1990. And shock-jock Howard Stern (with sidekick Robin Quivers), 40, called off his Libertarian Party run for governor of New York, because he didn't want to disclose his financials.

DUMPED INCUMBENTS & OTHER LOSERS

Thomas Foley, 65, 15-term Democratic Congressman from Washington and the first Speaker of the House ejected from his seat since 1860.

Dan Rostenkowski, 66, controversial Chicago Democratic machine pol, powerful chairman of the House Ways and Means Committee; after 36 years and 17 indictments.

Hugh Rodham, 44, a Miami public defender and younger brother of the First Lady, defeated by a humiliating 70% to 30% by Florida's Republican incumbent U.S. Senator, Connie Mack.

Mario Cuomo, 62, golden-throated Democratic Governor of New York and periodic shy suitor of a presidential nomination; after 12 years.

The number of incumbent Republican senators, representatives and governors who lost in the supposed Year of the Anti-Incumbent: None.

The ultimate loser if the '94 elections don't improve government performance: The shameless 61% of voting-age Americans who didn't vote.

PARTINGS

Some sundered as if for shock effect, like Tom and Roseanne, and some with rancor, like **DIANA** *and* **CHARLES,** *while others, like Martina Navratilova, left the field with grace*

IRRECONCILABLE DIFFERENCES

When the marriages of public figures go sour, they are often dragged through the headlines and bylines of the press with particularly tasteless glee. In 1994, the second year of their official separation, the union of the Prince and Princess of Wales seemed to unspool with a special savagery and at indecent length in every possible medium. Worse, Charles and the House of Windsor itself seemed to lose in the process the public sympathy they so desperately tried to engender.

The press was not entirely to blame: The principals fueled the fire themselves, cooperating with unseemly disclosures and partisan biographies about lovers old and new, alienation of feelings, eating disorders and suicide attempts. The accounts vacillated between emotional self-defense and the kind of stinging, never-quite-forgotten accusations that are offered up in divorce courts. Along the way, they allowed a blinding and unwelcome illumination of a British monarchy that had heretofore survived by keeping a stiff upper lip and a dogged reticence about its private affairs. And caught in this murderous crossfire, Charles and Diana found themselves the villains of a klieg-lit reality that had finally, and sadly, overtaken the soft-focus fairy tale.

An emotionally spent Diana, 33, announced at the end of 1993 that she would be leaving public life. As it happened, her startling decision to abandon most of her royal duties only added to her troubles. In '94, she became embroiled in a topless-photo scandal when a paparazzo caught her sunbathing in Spain. She was then accused of adultery with ex-Army officer James Hewitt, 36, whose story, recounted by Anna Pasternak in the shamelessly florid *Princess in Love*, detailed Hewitt's trysts with the Princess. Hewitt depicted her as contemplating leaving Charles for him. He even ungallantly claimed that she had had sex with him at the Waleses' country home, Highgrove (among other locales), while Princes William, 12, and Harry, 10, were in the next room.

Only weeks before these damaging revelations, Diana was linked with dashing millionaire Oliver Hoare, 48, a married London art dealer who had offered to act as go-between for the Waleses when their marriage was collapsing. He is said to have listened for hours as Diana poured out her sorrow and frustration. And she, wrote *News of the World*, had rung his Chelsea manse some 300 times over a period of 18 months beginning in 1992. Lonely and obsessive, she reportedly stayed on the line, saying nothing, while the anxious Hoare demanded, "Who's there? Who's there?" None of it was true, claimed Di. "What have I done to deserve this?" she asked friendly *Daily Mail* correspondent Richard Kay. "They are trying to make out that I was having an affair with this man...I feel I am being destroyed." There was more to come, including the bald declaration in *The Prince of Wales: A Biography* that theirs had been a loveless marriage. Meanwhile, her pragmatic royal in-laws continued to marginalize her image, but she still managed to maintain the balance of support from an endlessly patient public.

Behind the headlines, Diana was a woman adrift without the charity work that had sustained her. She filled her days with shopping, lunch dates and workouts. Keen on becoming a "real person," as she put it, she dismissed her bodyguards, and became vulnerable to curiosity seekers, as well as to always lurking photographers. She turned to discreet friends such as Lucia Flecha de Lima (wife of Brazil's ambassador to the U. S.) for comfort. By year's end, impatient with "retirement," she reentered public life via her work for the Red Cross—"returning to the things she does best," as a friend put it.

Meanwhile, the Prince of Wales became the Prince of Wails. Struggling to overcome his image as the diffident twit who allowed his marriage to founder, Charles, 45, rolled up his tailor-made sleeves and wrestled with the demon of publicity. First in a British TV documentary, *Charles, the Private Man, the Public Role*, and later in the sympathetic biography *Prince of Wales*, based on his diaries and letters, Charles worked closely with TV broadcaster Jonathan Dimbleby. The journalist cast him as an emotionally deprived pawn abandoned to nannies by Queen Elizabeth and bullied into a charade marriage by Prince Philip. After the press picked up Di's trail to Balmoral and Sandringham, Dimbleby suggests, the pressure to announce an engagement became unbearable. Charles, he says, "felt ill-used but impotent," and "interpreted his father's attitude as an ultimatum." Afterward, Charles was shocked, Dimbleby wrote, to find that Diana was desperate and depressed at the same time she was intoxicated by publicity and consumed by the notion that he was sleeping with his premarital paramour, Camilla Parker Bowles, 46, whose voice was heard on the notorious "Camillagate" tape in 1989. Charles maintained in his TV interview that he remained faithful to the most glamorous woman in Britain "until it became clear that the marriage had irretrievably broken down." (But another '94 tome, *Camilla: The King's Mistress*, claims that Charles spent the night before his wedding with Parker Bowles.)

In the beginning, Dimbleby writes, Charles blamed himself for Diana's woes: "He [told friends] that it was too much to expect anyone to be the wife of the heir to

the throne." By 1982, the Prince arranged for Diana to consult a psychiatrist, but the problems continued. "During bouts of unhappiness," writes Dimbleby, "she would sit hunched on a chair...quite inconsolable." In his diary, Charles lamented, "How awful incompatibility is, and how dreadfully destructive it can be...I never thought it would end up like this. How could I have got it all so wrong?" A more pressing question, however, is why Charles decided to parade his anguish before the world. By the end of the year, as lawyers for the principals were said to be working on their divorce agreement—arguing over such matters as whether Diana will keep her title—Charles's own rightness for the throne became debatable. Legally, nothing, including a divorce, bars him from ruling, but London's *Sun* newspaper spoke for many pained and perplexed Britons when it declared, "He has the upbringing, the dedication and the training. But he lacks the most vital qualification: the respect of his subjects."

Doin' the Windsor Shuffle: Royal watchers believe Charles wants to eventually wed Camilla Parker Bowles, married and the mother of two. But her husband Andrew Parker Bowles, 55, an Army brigadier and a Roman Catholic (at left with his wife), has said that divorce is not an option. Diana, meantime, was embarrassed in '94 by revelations about two men. She reportedly clung to Oliver Hoare (top right, at home in London with his wife Diane), a friend of the royal couple, who tried to play a Jimmy Carter role in the War of the Waleses. And the Princess was bitterly hurt when unemployed former Guards Captain James Hewitt (with Di in 1991) bragged, lucratively, in print about their "physical relationship."

SPLIT CITY

Was the L.A. earthquake or the bustup of Tom and Roseanne 1994's most seismic event? The Arnolds first hoaxed the media with talk of a "three-way marriage" with assistant Kim Silva (above). And not ones to tarry when their four-year match did die, Roseanne, 41, declared that she would wed an eery Arnold look-alike, her 240-lb. bodyguard-chauffeur, Ben Thomas (below), 28; and Tom, 35, was smitten with college student Julie Champnella, 21.

It was also the year of the quickie. This trio of pairs said yes, and no, in jet-setting time. Fastest off the mark was Bad Girls *costar Drew Barrymore (right), 19, who hit the trail from bar owner Jeremy Thomas, 31, after a mere 29 days. Ex-90210er Shannen Doherty (below right), 22, moved to a different zip code just five months after saying "I do" to Ashley Hamilton, 19; and Paula Abdul, 31, and Emilio Estevez, 32, cancelled their duet after 741 days.*

PARTINGS 1994

Syndicated newspaper columnist *Dave Barry*, 47, author of 13 humor books and the inspiration for the CBS sitcom *Dave's World*, and wife *Betty*, 47, a journalist; after 19 years and one son.

Smooth movie martial arts honcho *Steven (On Deadly Ground) Seagal*, 42, and former model *Kelly LeBrock,* 34; after seven years and three children.

Less-smooth movie martial arts actor *Jean-Claude Van Damme,* 32, and fourth wife *Darcy LaPier*, 28; after a mere nine months.

Comedian *Jerry Seinfeld,* 40, parted company with college-student girlfriend *Shoshanna Lonstein,* 19, after18 months. Her father Zachary said, "His career and her school were to blame."

PARTINGS 1994

Sharon Stone, 36, who last year dropped country heart-throb Dwight Yoakam for *Sliver* producer *Bill MacDonald*, 37, has since split with fiancé MacDonald.

Sylvester Stallone, 48, and *Jennifer Flavin*, 25, ended their relationship; he also parted company with his fiancée, model-photographer Janice Dickinson, 37, after a DNA test proved conclusively that Sly is not the father of her daughter Savannah Rodin.

Kathleen Kinmont, 28, and *Lorenzo Lamas*, 36, costars of the TV action series *Renegade*; after less than four years.

Intergalactic legend *William Shatner*, 62, and his wife, actress *Marcy Lafferty*, 47; after 20 years and no children.

Tonight Show bandleader *Branford Marsalis*, 33, and wife *Teresa*; after nine years and one son.

Environmental lawyer *Robert F. Kennedy Jr.*, 40, and attorney *Emily Black*, 37; after 12 years and two children.

Nick Nolte, 53, and *Rebecca Linger*, 35; after 10 years and one son.

Godfather of Soul *James Brown*, 61, legally separated from fourth wife *Adrienne*, 43.

Melanie Griffith (above), 37, divorced Don Johnson, 44, again—their second marriage lasted five years. The actress called it quits with Johnson when his drinking again landed him in rehab, and she (again) took to pills and alcohol to numb the pain of the relationship. Singer Phil Collins, 43, broke up a new-fangled way: he faxed his intentions to his wife of 10 years, Jill Tavelman, 38 (with them: daughter Lily, 5).

PARTINGS 1994

Prince Karim Aga Khan, 57, one of the world's richest men with a fortune estimated at $1.4 billion and worldwide leader of 15 million Shiite Ismaili Muslims, and his wife, former model *Sally Crocker-Poole*, 54; after 25 years of marriage and three children.

Former Chrysler chairman *Lee Iacocca*, 70, and *Darrien*, 45; after three years of marriage and no children. This was his third marriage, her second.

Singer-composer *Neil Diamond*, 53, and wife *Marcia*, 48; after 24 years and two sons.

Tony Curtis, 69, and fourth wife *Lisa Deutsch Curtis*, 32; after 17 months.

Guns N' Roses drummer *Matthew Sorum*, 33, and actress wife *Kai*, 25; after one year.

Model *Cindy Crawford*, 28, and actor *Richard Gere*, 45, separated after three years.

Sally Field, 47, filed for divorce from second husband *Alan Greisman*, 46, head of Savoy Pictures; after nine years and one child.

Actress *Diane Lane*, 29, filed for divorce from actor *Christopher Lambert*, 36; after six years and one child.

Actress *Melissa Gilbert*, 30, who had reconciled with actor *Bruce Boxleitner*, 44, in June, broke off her second engagement to him.

A month after her split from hubby of nine years Billy Joel, 45, supermodel Christie Brinkley, 40 (right, with their daughter Alexa, 8), announced her engagement to Los Angeles developer Rick Taubman, 45. And after 16 years and three children, Kevin Costner, 39, ended his marriage to Cindy, 38. Said he: "I try to conduct my life with a certain amount of dignity and discretion, but marriage is a hard, hard gig."

FADES & FLAMEOUTS

Some celebrity departees exited in '94 on a cloud of loftier ambitions, others on a chute of slipping ratings. But Hollywood's Splitee of the Year was Disney Studios genie Jeffrey Katzenberg, 44, who defected after CEO Michael Eisner, 52, had bypass surgery but refused to anoint him heir apparent. Katzenberg—whose reign had produced *Pretty Woman* and an animation revival at Disney—then shook the industry by launching a rival "dream-team" entertainment conglomerate with megamoguls Steven Spielberg and David Geffen.

That's Katzenberg (above, left) with Eisner in together times. Meanwhile, David Caruso, 38, copped out of mega-hit NYPD Blue *after being denied a meaty raise. As he limoed toward what may prove a lucrative screen career, he was smacked with a palimony suit by his ex-live-in of four years, actress Paris Papiro.*

Talk about swan songs: Tired of her prima-donna demands and undependability, the Metropolitan Opera unceremoniously dumped diva Kathleen Battle (left), 44. After raves for his role in the big screen Quiz Show, *Rob Morrow, 31, departed* Northern Exposure's *permafrost with relative affection following four seasons for more movie roles. And despite a vow to "kick Jay Leno's ass," Arsenio Hall, 37, gathered his final "woof" after five late-night years. "It was time," he says, "to move on."*

EGRESSING GRACE

In life timing is all, and not least in that final test of a public figure—knowing when to say adieu. Kansas City Royals third baseman George Brett set a standard of eloquence in 1993 when he ended a 20-year career, declaring, "The game had become a job for me, and I thought baseball deserved better than that." Perhaps that was the feeling of Martina Navratilova (below), tennis's greatest woman player and a champion of gay dignity, when she decided to step down at 38 in the year she nearly won a 10th Wimbledon singles title. The Czech native who once said, "I was born to be an American," was but one of her new countrymen who retired in 1994 with great good grace.

Chief Wilma Mankiller (above), 49, the first woman to lead the Cherokee Nation, decided that two four-year terms were enough; and CBS newsman and essayist Charles Kuralt, 59, an 11-Emmy winner, left the road after 37 years.

Justice Harry Blackmun (right), 85, who wrote the majority opinion in 1973's landmark Roe v. Wade, *guaranteeing a woman's right to a legal abortion, stepped down from the Supreme Court after 24 distinguished years. Paul "Red" Adair, 78, who flew out of his Houston base to blow out the world's most uncontrollable oil-well fires (including 119 in the Gulf War) and became the model for the 1969 John Wayne movie,* Hellfighters, *finally decided, after five decades, that he had taken enough heat.*

STEPPING DOWN 1994

Ryne Sandberg, 34, the Chicago Cubs All-Star second baseman, announced his retirement mid-season, citing his poor performance and his desire to spend more time with his wife and family. A week after his announcement, his wife, *Cynthia Diane*, filed for divorce.

The Far Side creator, *Gary Larson*, 44, gave up his syndicated cartoon (but not books) after 15 years, citing "simple fatigue and a fear my work will begin to suffer or at the very least ease into the Graveyard of Mediocre Cartoons."

After 29 Indy 500s, shelves full of auto racing trophies and over $10 million in prize money, *Mario Andretti*, 54, got out of the driver's seat. "I had a feeling the time was right," he said.

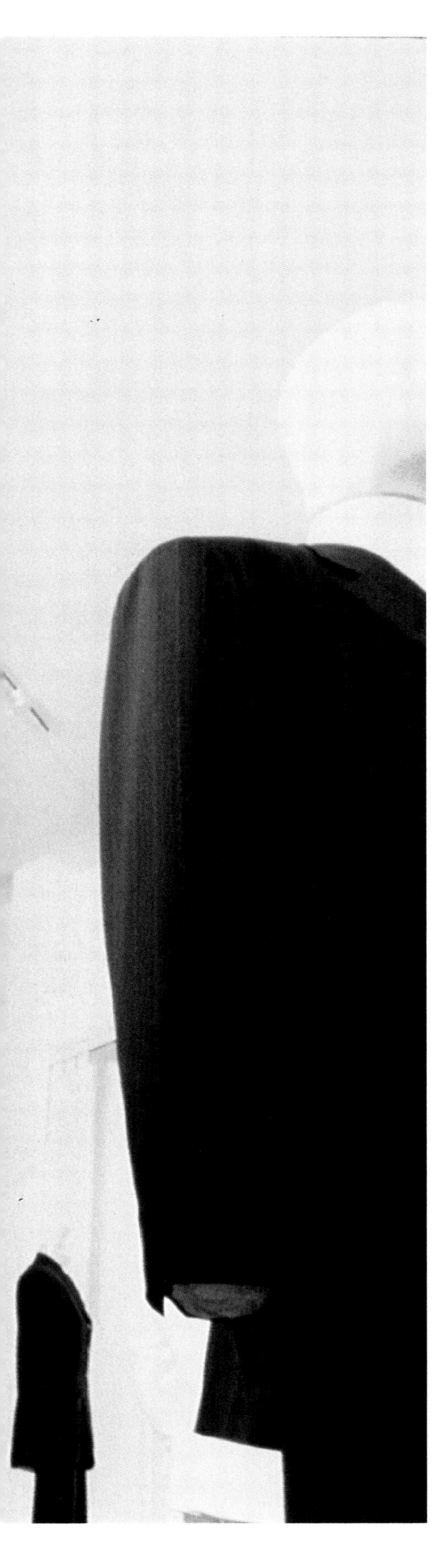

LOOK OF THE YEAR

Classic With A Twist

Less made more in '94: Wonderbras, see-thrus, slip dresses and the sleek drama of **RICHARD TYLER**

When Richard Tyler won the Council of Fashion Designers of America award as the hot discovery of the year, there was an undercurrent of irony. At 46, he is the oldest designer to win the industry's new-talent Oscar, but he's not at all new.

In fact, Tyler has been haute since 1988, when he and his wife, Lisa Trafficante, now 37, opened the Tyler Trafficante shop in L.A. and began dressing celebrities like Oprah, Susan Sarandon and Daryl Hannah. They made the gown Julia Roberts was to wear in her canceled wedding to Kiefer Sutherland. At last year's Oscars—usually a showcase for Armani duds—Roberts, Anjelica Huston and Diane Keaton showed up impeccably Tylered. Since then, Tyler has waded into the American mainstream, becoming design director of Anne Klein, the upmarket women's sportswear house. Thanks to what he calls his "classic with a twist, wearable but not boring" line, store orders jumped 30 percent. Says Ellin Saltzman, fashion director of Bergdorf Goodman: "These are not Prom Queen clothes."

The son of an Australian plastics factory foreman and a theatrical-costume designer, Tyler sold body-hugging sequined outfits with his mother at their Melbourne shop to the likes of Cher, Elton John and Alice Cooper. "It was more rock and roll than what I'm designing now," he says. Tyler wed Doris Taylor, who later became Rod Stewart's tour secretary. The marriage, which produced a son, Sheridan, now 17, failed after 10 years, and Tyler followed his clientele to London, then to L.A. in 1984. There he met actress and decorator-renovator Trafficante. Says Lisa: "He was shy, his hair hung in front of his face, but he had that passionate feeling about his work. We fell in love." Trafficante invested in his career, and business was soon so brisk that Richard didn't cut Lisa's wedding gown until 2 a.m. on the day of their marriage in 1989. Since the birth of their son, Edward Charles, a Tyler line for tiny tykes "seems inevitable," says the designer.

UNDER WEARERS

"The world is dying to know," 17-year-old Laetitia Thompson asked Bill Clinton during an MTV town hall meeting. "Is it boxers or briefs?" Clinton's response: "Usually briefs." From a look at the fashion polls, the President was in tune with the time. Briefness was boss from Beverly Hills to Broadway. We were, it seemed, one nation underdressed, with too much liberty for all. Maybe *The Mask* star, comedian Jim Carrey, spoke for many when asked for *his* preference. "I wear underwear, but just because I'm a conformist," he said. "I don't enjoy it."

Sometimes frumpy Daryl Hannah (above) this year gave 'em the slip (dress); actress Ellen Barkin was R-rated in Versace see-thru; and curve-making Wonderbras (on models below) lifted off from store racks—by the thousands.

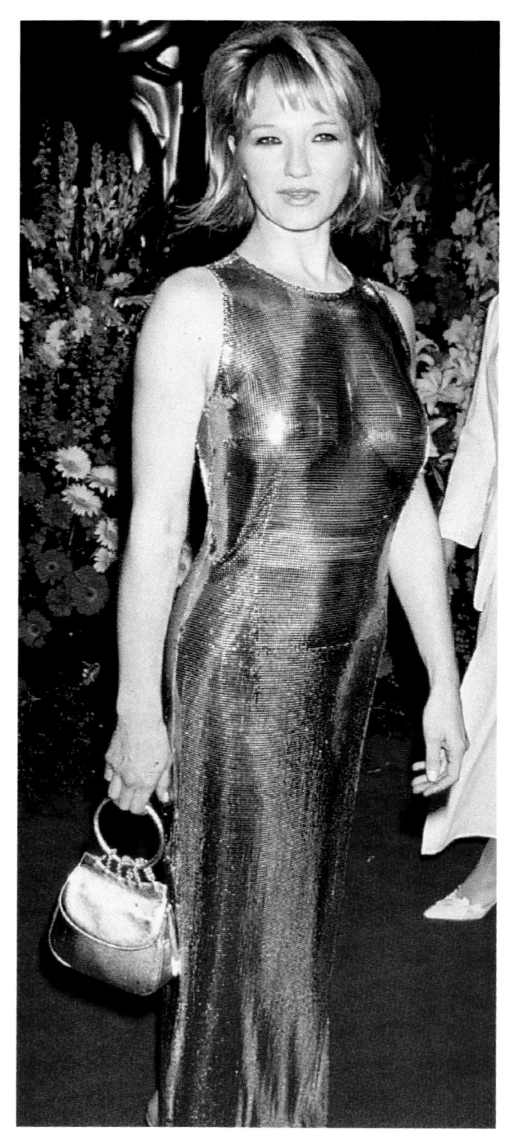

Well-muscled supermannequin of the moment Nadja Auermann (left), 23, sparkled in spangles at a spring show. The Berlin-born model's 5' 11½", 119-lb. frame waifed goodbye to last year's hungry, haunted look. Maybe that's why sunken-cheeked Kate Moss (in Anna Sui chains, right above) hid her eyes but bared her shallow navel. And why did Hugh Grant's voluptuously pinned up lady, Elizabeth Hurley, split her sides at the Oscars?

***PEOPLE*'S 10 BEST & WORST DRESSED OF 1994**

BEST DRESSED

Lloyd Bentsen, *73, Treasury Secretary*
Boyz II Men, *R&B quartet*
Daisy Fuentes, *27, veejay*
Hugh Grant, *33, actor*
Tom Hanks, *38, actor*
Heather Locklear, *32, actress*
Sarah Jessica Parker, *29, actress*
Barbra Streisand, *52, entertainer*
Tracey Ullman, *34, actress*
Barbara Walters, *62, newscaster*

WORST DRESSED

Christina Applegate, *22, actress*
Arquette Family (Rosanna, Patricia, David, Alexis), *show folk*
Brett Butler, *36, actress*
Hillary Rodham Clinton, *46, First Lady*
Duchess of York, *34*
Kim Fields, *25, actress*
Ethan Hawke, *23, actor*
Susan Lucci, *45, actress*
♀ (formerly Prince), *36, singer*
Howard Stern, *40, talk show host*

SARAHDIPITY

Fashion-wise, '94 had its fabs and its frumps. The 5' 4" costar of *Honeymoon in Vegas* and *Hocus Pocus*, Sarah Jessica Parker (above), 29, a self-described "eclectic dresser," stood tall and tasteful in Calvin Klein basic black. But Sarah Ferguson, 34, the dowdy duchess whose style sense is as off-and-on as her royal romance, suffered an acute case of static cling, prompting one London columnist to quip: "She has the knack of wearing clothes that never go out of style. They look just as ridiculous year after year."

ANTONIO BANDERAS

To hear him tell it, Antonio Banderas is one unlucky hombre. Never mind that the star of *The Mambo Kings*, who scorches screens opposite Tom Cruise in *Interview with the Vampire*, has reinvented the Latin Lover with verve and sensitivity. Tom Hanks, accepting a Golden Globe Award for *Philadelphia*, quipped of his onscreen mate, "To be in love with Antonio Banderas, I'm the envy of men and women all over the world." But Banderas, one of PEOPLE's 50 Most Beautiful, still thinks he is cursed, afflicted. "In Spain," explains the Málaga native, "we have a saying that translates to 'The uglier the man, the better.' " Still, Banderas, 33, who shares homes in Madrid and Manhattan with his wife, actress Ana Leza, avoids vanity. "I wake up every morning," he laughs, "look in the mirror and ask, 'Am I a sex symbol?' Then I go back to bed again."

PEOPLE'S 50 MOST BEAUTIFUL PEOPLE IN THE WORLD 1994

Kimberly Aiken, *18, Miss America '93*
Gabrielle Anwar, *24, actress*
Barbara Babcock, *57, actress*
Antonio Banderas, *33, actor*
Tyra Banks, *20, model*
Jill Barad, 42, *executive*
Juliette Binoche, *30, actress*
David Bouley, *40, chef*
Toni Braxton, *26, singer*
Ethan Browne, *20, model*
Darcey Bussell, *25, ballerina*
Dean Cain, *27, actor*
Valerie Campbell, *42, model*
David Caruso, *38, actor*
Henry Cisneros, *46, HUD Secretary*
Tom Cruise, *31, actor*
Daniel Day-Lewis, *37, actor*
Faye Dunaway, *53, actress*
Emme, *27, model*
Ralph Fiennes, *31, actor*
Ekaterina Gordeeva, *22, figure skater*
Al Gore Jr., *46, Vice President*
Hugh Grant, *33, actor*
Estelle Hallyday, *27, model*
John Harkes, *27, soccer player*
Dan Jansen, *28, speed skater*
Beverly Joubert, *37 , filmmaker*
Derek Joubert, 38, *filmmaker*
David Justice, *28, baseball player*
John F. Kennedy Jr., *33, lawyer*
Matt Lauer, *36, newscaster*
Joey Lawrence, *18, actor*
Heather Locklear, *32, actress*
Louise Lombard, *23, actress*
Nnenna Lynch, *22, runner*
John Michael Montgomery, *29, singer*
Julie Moran, *32, sportscaster*
Paul Newman, *69, actor*
Julia Roberts, *26, actress*
Meg Ryan, *32, actress*
Winona Ryder, *22, actress*
Antonio Sabato Jr., *22, actor*
Stephanie Seymour, *25, model*

They huddled, cuddled, mixed and matched. Among 1994's panting romantics were Rush and Whoopi and the unlikely likes of **MICHAEL** *and* **LISA MARIE**

THE PRINCESS WEDS THE KING

Holy Vow! Neverland met Graceland at the altar. It was hard to imagine how our unstable world, which witnessed the evisceration of the 35-year-old singer's career by accusations of child molestation, was going to accommodate the notion. But on August 1, Lisa Marie, 26, Elvis Presley's only child, confirmed the whispers that had been swirling for weeks. "My married name is Mrs. Lisa Marie Presley-Jackson," she said in an announcement, issued three weeks after a Dominican Republic judge produced a marriage license bearing the couple's signatures. "My marriage to Michael Jackson took place in a private ceremony outside the United States. I am very much in love with Michael. I dedicate my life to being his wife. I understand and support him. We both look forward to raising a family." Of course, Presley-Jackson brought to the marriage two children: Danielle, 5, and Benjamin, 22 months, her daughter and son by her first husband, rock bassist Danny Keough, 29, whom she married in 1988 and divorced in 1994.

As a couple they *are* kind of hard to reconcile. On one side of the aisle was the 5' 3" Graceland heiress, who has her father's sensuous mouth, a $150 million estate that likely will be completely hers at age 30 and an unswerving faith in the controversial Church of Scientology. On the other side, there is the 5' 10" but perpetually waiflike, notoriously germ-phobic, curio-at-large Jackson. The singer, who seems never to have had a serious romantic relationship, was still under investigation by L.A. and Santa Barbara authorities for allegedly molesting a now 14-year-old boy. (The civil portion of the case was settled when Jackson paid the child a reported $15 to $20 million in damages.)

The families of the bride and groom have not exactly been gushing forth their approval. Jackson's parents, Joe and Katherine, and his siblings, Rebbie, Jackie, Tito, Jermaine, LaToya, Marlon, Randy and Janet, had no immediate comment about Michael's marriage, but Johnnie L. Cochran, Jr., one of O.J. Simpson's lawyers who represented Michael in the molestation case, says that those in his inner circle "are happily surprised." Lisa Marie's mother, Priscilla, 48, who attended her daughter's first marriage but not her second, said through her publicist that she is "very supportive of everything Lisa Marie does." But one source close to the Presley camp says Priscilla "looked downright terrible. It was obvious she was very preoccupied."

Buck up, Mom. Michael was reportedly writing three songs for Lisa Marie and adding them to his next album, *History*, a greatest-hits collection due in 1995. Besides, there must be *some* way to make sense of this marriage. One suggestion: Their lifestyles are compatible, says David Adler, coauthor of the 1990 unauthorized paperback bio of Lisa Marie, *Elvis' Daughter*. Like Michael, says Adler, Presley's only child is "reclusive and idiosyncratic." (Favorite place to shop: the Dart Rexall drugstore in L.A.) And their celebrity synchronicity is undeniable. "Lisa Marie's mother married the most famous singer of her time," says Adler of the 1967 marriage between Presley and 20-year-old Priscilla, "and now Lisa Marie has married the most famous singer of her era." Says Washington attorney John Coale, Lisa Marie's friend: "I guess she and Michael are our rock and roll royalty."

GOIN' TO THE CHAPEL

Do you take this woman? And do you take this man? Did they ever! From Broadway to Beverly Hills, crooners and comedians, designers and Deadheads, actors, athletes, politicians, models and an ex-madam helped make the year a star-studded altarcation, while some others merely—but loudly—announced their intentions to march down the aisle. Cutting a cake in the shape of her million-dollar diamond and sapphire ring, Ivana Trump (right), 45, celebrated her engagement to entrepreneur Riccardo Mazzucchelli, 51. Meanwhile, her ex-husband , Donald, 47, tied the knot with actress Marla Maples, 30. The ceremony began late because the bride had to breast-feed the couple's 2-month-old daughter, Tiffany.

Winning her struggle against anorexia, actress Tracey Gold, 25 (above with groom Roby Marshall, 29), had her wedding cake—and ate it too. In a rural New York church, the Redgrave family's Natasha Richardson (below, right), 31, linked with Schindler's List's *Liam Neeson, 42; crooner Harry Connick Jr., 26, did the love/marriage, horse/carriage bit with model Jill Goodacre, 30.*

WEDDINGS 1994

Oscar emcee and comic actress *Whoopi Goldberg*, 44, and movie and TV technicians' union organizer *Lyle Trachtenberg*, 40, at the bride's Pacific Palisades home before 350 A-list guests. They met last year on the set of *Corrina, Corrina*.

Software billionaire *Bill Gates*, 38, and Microsoft executive *Melinda French*, 29, in a $1 million Hawaiian do.

Singer *Wayne Newton*, 52, and lawyer *Kathleen McCrone*, 30, in Las Vegas, of course.

First Brother *Roger Clinton*, 37, and eight-months-pregnant *Molly Martin*, 25. (The President served as best man.)

Action hero *Jean-Claude Van Damme*, 32, and *Darcy LaPier*, 28.

Grateful Dead's lead guitarist and necktie designer *Jerry Garcia*, 51, and *Deborah Koons*, a 40ish filmmaker.

Princess Margaret's daughter, *Sarah Armstrong-Jones*, 30, and fellow artist *Daniel Chatto*, 37.

Actor *Edward James Olmos*, 46, and *Lorraine Bracco*, 39, actress ex of Harvey Keitel.

Country diva Trisha Yearwood (above), 29, wore the pants (by Richard Tyler) at her nuptials to Mavericks' bass player Robert Reynolds, 32. Model Anna Nicole Smith (right), 26, wed Texas oilman J.Howard Marshall II, 89. Arthurian *legend Dudley Moore, 59, married Nicole Rothschild, 30, attended by her son Chris.*

WEDDINGS 1994

90210's *Jennie Garth*, 22, and musician *Dan Clark*, 25. The couple met two years ago when Garth saw Clark perform at an L.A. coffeehouse.

Environmental lawyer *Robert F. Kennedy Jr.*, 40, and designer *Mary Richardson*, 34.

French singer *Johnny Hallyday*, 50, remarried his third wife, *Adeline Blondiau*, 23, two years after their divorce. The couple first married in 1990.

Actor *Lou Diamond Phillips*, 32, and model *Kelly Preston*, 26. (The bride, needless to say, is not the Kelly Preston married to John Travolta.)

Former model and (Gary) Hartbreaker *Donna Rice*, 36, and governmental consultant *Jack Hughes*, 42.

First Brother-in-Law *Tony Rodham*, 39, a regional coordinator for the Democratic National Committee, and *Nicole Boxer*, 26, a film-studio executive and daughter of Senator Barbara Boxer of California.

New York Republican Congresspeople *Susan Molinari*, 36, and *Bill Paxon*, 40.

All My Children actress *Teresa Blake*, 30, and Shenandoah drummer *Mike McGuire*, 35.

Homicide detective *Clark Johnson*, 37, and ex-model *Heather Salmon*, 30.

Richard (John Boy) *Thomas*, 43, and Santa Fe art dealer *Georgina Bischoff*, 34. His four (and her two) children from previous marriages attended.

L.A. Law*man Blair Underwood (above), 30, startled the 350 guests at his ceremony by galloping in on horseback while his talent cooordinator bride Désirée DaCosta, 29, was demurely reined in. Merging acts and assets, impressionist Rich Little, 55 (impersonating one of his faves, right) and Marilyn-esque comedian Jeannette Markey, 28, entertained guests with quips. "I didn't know whether to marry her or adopt her as a playmate for Bria," said Little, referring to his 17-year-old daughter from a previous marriage.*

WEDDINGS 1994

Supermodel *Niki Taylor*, 19, and *Matt Martinez*, 24, former linebacker for football's Miami Hooters.

Cranberries lead singer *Dolores O'Riordan*, 22, and *Don Burton*, 32, assistant tour manager for Duran Duran. The groom arrived on a black stallion, the bride in a horse-drawn cart.

Sliver screenwriter *Joe Eszterhas*, 49, and artist *Naomi Baka*, 35. (Baka's first husband, *Sliver* producer Bill MacDonald, ran off with the film's star, Sharon Stone; they subsequently broke up.)

Former Mayflower Madam *Sydney Biddle Barrows*, 42, and TV producer *Darnay Hoffman*, 46. Barrows wore pink, she says, because "with my age and history, wearing white would have been ludicrous."

Jason Robert Hervey, 22, Wayne of *The Wonder Years*, and socialite *Kelley Patricia O'Neill*, 27.

Lightning Jack star *Cuba Gooding*, 26, and teacher's aide *Sara Kapfer*, 24.

Allison Arngrim, 32, Nellie in *Little House on the Prairie*, and AIDS hotline colleague *Robert Schoonover*, 44.

Mad About You actress *Leila Kenzel*, 33, and acting coach *Neil Monaco*, 34. Their reception was held at a Burbank, Calif. bowling alley.

Twice divorced radio wind machine Rush Limbaugh (above), 43, wed journalist Marta Fitzgerald, 35, at the home of Supreme Court Justice Clarence Thomas. Model Claudia Schiffer (left), 23, kept magically showing up beside illusionist David Copperfield, 37, but he didn't produce a ring; and Britain's Prince Edward, 29, who had disappointed Fleet Street by his inactive or discreet romantic life, began dating Di look-alike P.R. woman Sophie Rhys-Jones, 29. Proclaimed a tabloid: "Well Done, My Son!"

Splendiferously lei-ed, Dustin Hoffman, 57, took his wife Lisa, 40, and their four kids (aged 7 to 14) by surprise when he arranged for them to renew their 1980 vows in a remote village on an island near Tahiti during a Pacific vacation.

WEDDINGS 1994

Former MTV Sports host and Burger King pitchman ("I love this place!") *Dan Cortese*, 26, and actress *Dee Dee Hemby*, 26.

Ringling Bros. and Barnum & Bailey Circus dancer *Marissa Young*, 24, and clown *Matt Richardson*, 21, wed under the Big Top before an audience of 6,000.

Actor *Joe Pantoliano*, 41, and model *Nancy Sheppard*, 31. His 13-year-old was best man, her eight-year-old the maid of honor.

Action actor *Dolph Lundgren*, 34, and *Anette Qviberg*, 20ish.

Brazilian soccer legend *Pelé*, 53, and psychologist *Assiria Lemos*, 36.

Pearl Jam's *Eddie Vedder*, 29, and writer *Beth Liebling*, 27. He wore a suit.

Daniel Roebuck, 30, *Matlock*'s Cliff Lewis, and former bookkeeper *Kelly Durst*, 24.

The Courtship of Eddie's Father actor *Brandon Cruz*, 32, and actress *Elizabeth Finklestein*, 26, who fell for him when she saw him on *Geraldo*.

Ice-skating stars *Jill Trenary*, 26, and *Christopher Dean*, 36.

As the World Turns actress *Martha Byrne*, 24, and New York City policeman *Michael McMahon*, 27.

Look Who's Nesting

"I can't imagine what life would be without Jett," says John Travolta (right), 40, about the 2-year-old son he has with his actress wife, Kelly Preston, 32. His words echo 1994's reigning celebrity sentiment. Hollywood went so overboard for family values that, along with the regulation-issue bottle of Evian, babies went everywhere with their parents. They were strolled into Spago, backpacked around Aspen and bundled around the Big Apple by doting stars. Travolta—who discoed in *Saturday Night Fever*, doo-wopped in *Grease*, and put an odd foot forward in this year's critically acclaimed *Pulp Fiction*—now romps in his Beverly Hills backyard, singing the "Barney" theme with Jett. We kid you not.

Kenny G. (left), 38, of saxophone-lite fame, kept 2-month-old son Maxwell from the New York City chill, and Mrs. Rod Stewart, Rachel Hunter, 25, cuddled 15-day-old son Liam, preparing him for his first—but certainly not last—ride on the Concorde.

Down for the count: after KOing Evander Holyfield for the heavyweight title, boxer Michael Moorer, 27, said, "I can't wait to be with my son." He flew home to snooze with 20-month-old Michael Jr. After his brief reign was dramatically ended, one fight later, by George Foreman, Moorer said, "The only thing that hurts is that, talking to my son, he was crying." Heavy lifting: Although she was turning letters on Wheel of Fortune *four months after the birth of son Nicholas, Vanna White, 37, a.k.a. Mrs. George Santo Pietro, may take another pregnancy leave. "Are you kidding?" she says. "I'm married to an Italian!"*

BIRTHS 1994

Bruce Springsteen, 44, and *Patti Scialfa*; 37; son Sam Ryan.

Tennis ace *Boris Becker*, 26, and actress-model *Barbara Feltus*, 27; son Noah Gabriel.

Skid Row lead singer *Sebastian Bach*, 25, and *Maria*, 30; son, London Siddhartha Halford.

Bruce Willis, 38, and *Demi Moore*, 31; daughter Tallulah Belle.

The Bold and the Beautiful's *Kimberlin Brown*, 32, and entrepreneur *Gary Pelzer*, 40; daughter Alexes Marie.

Donna Harris Lewis, 29, widow of basketball star *Reggie Lewis*; daughter Reggiena Sarah. Donna had learned of her pregnancy on the same July, 1993, day that Reggie died of cardiac arrest.

Model *Kim Alexis*, 34, and former hockey player *Ron Duguay*, 36; son Noah Fernand.

Mötley Crüe's *Nikki Sixx*, 35, and *Brandi*, 25; daughter Storm Brieann.

Rocker *John Mellencamp*, 42, and model *Elaine Irwin*, 24; son Ilud.

Kirstie Alley, 39, and *Parker Stevenson*, 42; daughter Lillie Price, by adoption.

Rolling Stones bassist *Bill Wyman*, 57, and *Suzanne*, 34; daughter Katharine Noelle.

Warren Beatty, 57, and *Annette Bening*, 36; a son (name not released).

BIRTHS 1994

Country crooner *Garth Brooks*, 32, and *Sandy*, 28; daughter August Anna.

Singer *Anita Baker*, 35, and land developer *Walter Bridgforth*, 36; son Edward Carlton.

Billy Ray Cyrus, 32, and *Leticia*, 27; son Braison Chance.

Gabrielle Carteris, 32, and stockbroker *Charles Isaacs*, 34; daughter Kelsey Rose.

Mikhail Baryshnikov, 46, and ex-ballerina *Lisa Rinehart,* 34; daughter Sofia-Luisa.

LeVar Burton, 37, and makeup artist *Stephanie*, 40; daughter Michaele Jean.

Princess Stéphanie of Monaco, 28, and boyfriend *Daniel Ducruet*, 28; daughter Pauline, the second out-of-wedlock child for the rambunctious princess and her former bodyguard.

Actor *Judd Hirsch*, 59, and fashion designer *Bonni*, 35; daughter Montana Eve.

Spike Lee, 37, and *Tonya Lewis*, 33; daughter Satchel.

TV's *Geraldo Rivera*, 51, and TV producer *C.C. Dyer*, 37; daughter Simone Cruickshank.

Eddie Murphy, 32, and wife *Nicole*, 26; daughter Shayne Audra.

Entertainment Tonight co-host *John Tesh*, 41, and actress *Connie Selleca*, 38; daughter Prima Sellecchia, while his CD, *Sax by the Fire*, played in the delivery room.

Adult children had pains and pleasures in '94. Fidel Castro's daughter and one of his sharpest critics, Alina Fernández (above), 37, defected to the U.S., leaving her own daughter in Cuba; psychotherapist Judy Lewis, 58, the love child of Clark Gable and Loretta Young (who had told Judy she was adopted), wrote a heartbreaking account of her parental discovery, Uncommon Knowledge.

It was the Shula Bowl: For the first time in the history of pro sports, a father and son (above) faced each other as coaches. When the final whistle blew, the Miami Dolphins of NFL fixture Don Shula, 64, defeated 35-year-old son David's Cincinnati Bengals 23-7. Then came the Shaq Attack: "Yo, yo. I want to dedicate this song to Phillip Arthur Harrison 'cause he was the one who took me from a boy to a man," raps NBA star Shaquille O'Neal, 22, in his song dissing his real father for abandoning the family. O'Neal (with his substitute dad, Harrison, left), performed "Biological Didn't Bother" on his album, Shaq-Fu: Da Return.

BIRTHS 1994

Chris Evert, 39, and former Olympic skier *Andy Mill*, 41; son Nicholas Joseph.

Jan DeBoer, 41, and wife *Roberta*, 36, the Michigan couple who lost the custody battle for their adopted daughter (known as Baby Jessica); son Casey Mitchell, by adoption.

Actor *John Schneider*, 40, and *Elly*, 28; daughter Karis Lynn.

Michelle Pfeiffer, 36, and *Picket Fences'* creator *David Kelley*, 38; son John Henry.

Actress *Katey Sagal*, 38, and drummer *Jack White*; daughter Sarah Grace.

General Hospital's Virginia Madsen, 32, and *Antonio Sabato Jr.*, 22; son Jack Antonio.

Actress *Mimi Rogers*, 39, and TV and film producer *Chris Ciaffa*, 31; daughter Lucy Julia.

Duran Duran's *Simon Le Bon*, 35, and *Yasmin*, 35; a daughter (name not released).

Producer *Norman Lear*, 72, and wife *Lyn*, 47, a psychologist (using a surrogate mother); twin daughters Madeline Rose and Brianna Elizabeth.

Gillian Anderson, 26, of *The X-Files*, and *Errol Clyde Klotz*, 33, daughter Piper.

Singer *Gloria Estefan*, 37, and manager-husband *Emilio*, 41; daughter Emily.

Actress *Sean Young*, 35, and *Robert Lujan*, 35; son Rio Kelly.

NBC correspondent *Faith Daniels*, 37, and CBS News exec *Dean Daniels*; daughter Aiden Rose, by adoption.

GOODBYES

We bid a fond farewell to the luminaries who left us in '94—from Jacqueline Onassis to

KURT COBAIN

BETTER TO BURN OUT...

"It's not fun for me anymore. I can't live this life," wrote Kurt Cobain, the drug-plagued rocker who hated to be called the voice of a generation, shortly before committing suicide with a shotgun. No matter how uncomfortable his status made him, the act left a generation grappling with troubling emotions of its own. "Now he's gone and joined that stupid club," said his mother, Wendy O'Connor, alluding to the pantheon of rockers—Janis Joplin, Jim Morrison and Jimi Hendrix—who all had died, like Cobain, at 27.

Like theirs too, Cobain's rise was meteoric. The Aberdeen, Washington, youth fell into a life of drugs and petty crime, working as a janitor at the high school where he dropped out. But making searing music with his alternative grunge band Nirvana on the Seattle scene seemed to focus his anger and angst. After the group's 1991 album, *Nevermind*, sold more than 10 million copies worldwide, however, he never quite recovered. In torn clothes, hacked-off hair and soaring on a heroin addiction punctuated with life-threatening overdoses, Cobain defined Generation X's alienation. Sometimes, he could laugh at his own ambivalence—"Teenage angst has paid off well," he sang in the opening cut of Nirvana's last album, *In Utero*.

After he married Hole lead singer Courtney Love in 1992 (their daughter Frances Bean was born six months later), his life seemed to find a lighter groove. But in the end, the humor that tempered the fury of his art, and the newfound happiness brought by the birth of the baby he adored, deserted him. Pain, it seemed, was all that remained. He admired Neil Young's lyric, "Better to burn out than fade away." Says Ray Manzarek, 59, the ex-Doors keyboardist who had watched Jim Morrison self-destruct, "Kurt was a poet. He didn't speak for his generation. He spoke for himself. That's what poets do."

MICHAEL O'DONOGHUE

One of the original writers and cast members of *Saturday Night Live*, Michael O'Donoghue, 54, was responsible for many of the show's most memorable and mordant skits. His irreverent and scatological comedy writing won Emmys in 1976 and 1977. He also worked on-camera, usually as Mr. Mike, who told twisted bedtime stories and liked to stick needles in his eyes. The character was featured in his 1979 film *Mr. Mike's Mondo Video*. O'Donoghue, who died of a massive cerebral hemorrhage at a New York City hospital, was married to Cheryl Hardwick, a music coordinator for *SNL*.

CAB CALLOWAY

A flamboyant bandleader and scat singer, Cab Calloway, 86, became an American musical icon for younger generations. He rose to fame as the "Hi-de-hi-de-hi-de-ho" man in the 1930s and '40s. Calloway, who died of complications from a stroke in a nursing home in Hockessin, Delaware, conducted his jazz band with a maniacal flair that contributed as much to his reknown as the music itself. His band, which performed at Harlem's famed Cotton Club, was featured in movies as well, including 1958's *St. Louis Blues*, with Nat King Cole and Eartha Kitt. Calloway was also a founder of the scat jazz style, which uses meaningless syllables instead of words. "He just loved performing," says Chicago music historian Howard Reich. "By sheer charisma, he proved that sophisticated jazz can also be great popular music." Calloway is further remembered for popularizing the zoot suit and coining the terms "jitterbug" and "copacetic." He appeared in *The Blues Brothers* (1980), in Janet Jackson's music video *Alright* (1990) and, not least, on *Sesame Street*.

DINAH SHORE

When Dinah Shore began to sing, you could almost smell the chicken fryin.' And no wonder. This daughter of a Nashville store owner had a Jewish cantor for a granduncle and a black nanny who took her to gospel services. Blessed with that heritage, she became one of the most popular female vocalists of the big-band era and a ray of sunshine in America's living rooms. Her Emmy-winning TV career (beginning with *The Dinah Shore Show* in 1951 and other talk and variety shows during the next 40 years) delightfully displayed her homespun charm. "Live TV has that little element of human fallibility," she once said. "If you make a mistake, you can use that old hambone and capitalize on it."

Equally upbeat offscreen, she was a renowned Beverly Hills hostess and an avid golfer. Her Dinah Shore Classic tournament was a fixture on the LPGA tour. In 1943, she married actor George Montgomery, now 77, and had daughter Melissa Ann Hime, 46, and adopted a son, John David Montgomery, 40. (They divorced in 1962.) Shore's subsequent marriage to contractor Maurice Smith lasted less than a year. But she wasn't finished with romance. In the '70s, she fell hard for Burt Reynolds, 19 years her junior, after he appeared on her show. Their May-December affair was the stuff of headlines and heartbreak. "He was the love of her life," says her chum, Lee Minnelli, widow of director Vincente Minnelli. "When he left her for a younger woman, Sally Field [in 1976], she was devastated." And when she died of ovarian cancer at 76, Reynolds was also bereft. She was, he said, Hollywood's "greatest and only angel. Dinah was the most wonderful friend I ever had." No one was finah.

GOODBYES 1994

Albert Goldman, 66, former music columnist who wrote controversial, unauthorized biographies of Lenny Bruce, Elvis Presley and John Lennon; of a heart attack.

British actor turned animal-rights activist *Bill Travers*, best known for his role as the lion-loving game warden George Adamson in *Born Free*; in his sleep at 72.

Rep. William Natcher, 84, iron-man Kentucky Democrat whose 18,401 consecutive congressional votes put him in the *Guinness Book of Records*; of heart and lung ailments.

Brazilian *Ayrton Senna*, 34, considered the top formula-one driver in the world; of head injuries after he hit a wall at 185 mph, during the San Marino Grand Prix in Imola, Italy.

Roland Ratzenberger, 31-year-old Austrian driver at the same San Marino Grand Prix qualifying round; of head injuries after crashing into a concrete barrier.

DOROTHY COLLINS

For eight years in the '50s, Dorothy Collins was America's singing sweetheart on the high-rated TV show *Your Hit Parade.* The Windsor, Ontario, native, who died of a heart attack at age 67, was noted for her girl-next-door demeanor and renditions of chart-topping tunes like "Shrimp Boats." In the '60s, she appeared frequently on Alan Funt's *Candid Camera.* Twice divorced (once from *Hit Parade* bandleader Raymond Scott) and the mother of three daughters, she exulted in her prim and perky image, saying, "That's me. You can't be what you aren't."

LINUS PAULING

Equal parts scientist and humanist, Linus Pauling, who died of prostate cancer at age 93, was a maverick who combined sheer intellect with charisma. He was the only person to receive two unshared Nobel Prizes—one in 1954 for his work on how atoms bond to form molecules, and another in 1962 for his efforts to prevent nuclear proliferation. Indeed, he remained a vocal critic of his profession. "Most problems in the modern world are the result of the contributions of science," he once said. On the day in 1962 when he and other Nobel laureates were to dine with President Kennedy, he spent the afternoon picketing the White House to end nuclear testing. Pauling was also a controversial advocate of vitamin C, which he said would ward off colds if taken in massive doses, as well as help fight heart disease and cancer. "I say my ideas are invaluable," he explained. "But they're not so obviously valuable that they're immediately accepted."

WILLIAM CONRAD

William Conrad, who died of cardiac arrest at 73, made no apologies for his grumpy, ground-hugging presence. Joe Penny, his slender *Jake and the Fatman* costar, once suggested that the 5'9" actor, who usually packed anywhere between 230 and 270 lbs., should go on a diet. Conrad put it to him: "Does a guy like me need a 32-inch waist? *No!* I feel sorry for a poor bastard like you. You got size 44 shoulders. Great-lookin'. You can't afford to have a cookie."

Conrad's appeal was shrink-proof. "People accepted him as the gruff, rough curmudgeon. Underneath, he was just a nice man," says former CBS executive Fred Silverman, who cast Conrad in two top-rated series, *Cannon* (1971-76) and *Fatman* (1987-92). But heft was only half his presence: His resonant voice also narrated TV's *Bullwinkle* cartoons and *The Fugitive*. That voice launched the Kentucky native onto the radio in the '40s. By his own reckoning, his résumé included 7,500 jobs, including Marshal Matt Dillon on the original *Gunsmoke*. He always loved mouthing off. "*Cannon* was crap," he groused after the show's run. "I was delighted to see it canceled." The snarl was far worse than the bite. He lived quietly with wife Tippy, widow of NBC newsman Chet Huntley. (He had a son, Christopher, 37, by first wife Susie, who died in 1979.) Says Tippy: "He wasn't concerned about whether he was successful or not. He just had a strong notion about what he wanted, and he went ahead and did it."

GOODBYES 1994

Photographer *Kevin Carter*, 33, who won this year's Pulitzer Prize for having hauntingly recorded a starving Sudanese child stalked by a vulture; an apparent suicide.

Paul Anderson, 61, Olympic gold medalist once recognized as the "world's strongest man" and in 1957 listed in the *Guinness Book of World Records* for lifting 6,270 pounds. For the last 33 years he ran a home for juvenile delinquents in Georgia; of complications from kidney failure.

Benito Agrelo, 15, Florida boy born with a malfunctioning liver, who won the right to refuse treatment to keep his body from rejecting a liver transplant because he no longer wanted to deal with the pain and side effects. His decision was supported by a circuit court.

Tournament-winning golfer *Bert Yancey*, who died of a heart attack at 56, left a promising career on the links in 1976 after a series of bizarre incidents, including arriving in Japan for a tournament and proclaiming himself a messiah ready to rid Japan of communism. Later diagnosed as suffering from manic depression, he rejoined the Senior Tour in 1988.

Mildred Natwick

Before her death at 89, Mildred Natwick was a versatile stage, TV and screen actress who was nominated for a Best Supporting Actress Oscar for 1967's *Barefoot in the Park*, opposite Robert Redford and Jane Fonda (left). Born in Baltimore, Natwick appeared in some 40 Broadway productions, receiving Tony nominations for 1957's *Waltz of the Toreadors* and 1971's *70, Girls, 70* (in which she made her singing debut at age 62). She also picked up an Emmy for the 1973-74 NBC series *The Snoop Sisters*, in which she and Helen Hayes played mystery writers solving real crimes.

Wilma Rudolph

With the long, graceful strides that were her signature, Wilma Rudolph became the first American woman to win three gold medals in a single Olympics, the 1960 Rome Games. The 20th of 22 children reared by a Tennessee railroad porter and his second wife, Rudolph, who died of brain cancer at 54, was struck in childhood with scarlet fever and polio. Doctors said she would never walk again, but with her mother's physical therapy, plus hospital heat treatments, she recovered to become a basketball star at 13. At Tennessee State University, she joined the legendary Tigerbelles track team, which has produced 40 women Olympians. For her victory lap in life, she worked as coach, teacher and goodwill ambassador to West Africa. In 1981, Rudolph, who was married twice and had four children, founded a nonprofit foundation in her name to help disabled children. "She was born to do more in the world than run on the track," says Olympic teammate Isabelle Daniels Holston. "She was born to inspire, to love and to give."

RAUL JULIA

From Don Quixote to Gomez Addams, Aristotle Onassis to Mack the Knife, Shakespeare to *Sesame Street*, Raul Julia brought flair and fire to an astonishing range of screen and stage roles. Julia, who had been battling cancer, died in a Long Island, New York, hospital after suffering a massive stroke. He was 54.

Though his box-office peak was as Gomez (above), the smoldering patriarch of the Addams Family movies, Julia was an actor for all seasonings. A strapping 6' 2", with heavy-lidded brown eyes that radiated sensuality and a resonant voice that carried traces of his native Puerto Rico, he moved easily among leading roles in Broadway musicals (*Man of La Mancha*, *The Threepenny Opera*), the Bard (*Othello*, *The Taming of the Shrew*) and films (*Kiss of the Spider Woman*, *Presumed Innocent*). He even played a convincingly diminutive Onassis in the 1988 TV miniseries *The Richest Man in the World*.

Born Raúl Rafael Carlos Juliá y Arcelay in San Juan, to a restaurateur and his homemaker wife, Julia moved to Manhattan at age 22 but had difficulty landing parts until producer Joseph Papp took him under his wing at the New York Shakespeare Festival. He earned the first of four Tony nominations in Papp's musical version of Shakespeare's *Two Gentlemen of Verona* in 1971, the same year he appeared on *Sesame Street* as Rafael the Fixit Man, a role that endeared him to yet another generation.

Julia, who had been married previously, wed dancer Merel Poloway in 1976. They had two sons, Raul Sigmund, 11, and Benjamin Rafael, 7. "Raul's family," says good friend Edward James Olmos, "filled his heart."

GOODBYES 1994

Popular *Good Morning America* veterinarian *Stephen Kritsick*, 42, who announced on-air in 1993 that he was gay and HIV-positive; of AIDS-related lymphoma.

University of Oklahoma football coach *Bud Wilkinson*, 77, who guided the Sooners to three national championships and a record 47 straight wins in the '50s; of congestive heart failure.

Italian actress *Giulietta Masina*, 73, widow of director Federico Fellini and costar of his 1954 film *La Strada*; of lung cancer.

British actor *David Langton*, 82, best known as Lord Bellamy in the phenomenally popular PBS series *Upstairs, Downstairs*; of a heart attack.

Gaunt character actor *Royal Dano*, 71, who costarred in more than 100 movies and played a memorable Abe Lincoln in the early 1950s on CBS's *Omnibus*; of pulmonary fibrosis.

Rabbi Menachem Mendel Schneerson, 92, head of one of the world's largest Hasidic Jewish communities, with an estimated 250,000 followers worldwide and believed by some of them to be the Messiah; of complications from a stroke.

TELLY SAVALAS

As a potential superstar, he should have been a tough sell, lacking as he was in hair, muscle tone and classic features. A lollipop seemed lodged permanently in one corner of his mouth, and he greeted everyone with a husky "Who loves ya, baby?" But some inexplicable combination of telegenics and testosterone made Aristotle "Telly" Savalas, who died of bladder cancer at the age of 72, a small-screen icon—and an improbable sex symbol. "He was like Sinatra," says actress Angie Dickinson. "When you walked into a room with him, you knew everybody was looking at *him*." Savalas had another explanation for his appeal: "I'm the kind of gorilla that people can identify with."

After three years in the Army during World War II, he earned a degree in psychology at Columbia University and worked for the Voice of America before turning to acting. Burt Lancaster saw him on the CBS series *The Witness* and gave him a role in his 1961 movie *The Young Savages*. The next year, he won an Oscar nomination for *Birdman of Alcatraz* and went on to appear in numerous other films, including *The Dirty Dozen*.

But it was *Kojak* that made him a phenomenon. He was already 51 in 1973 when he took on the role of the dapper police detective, and alchemized from gritty character actor to pop-cultural hero. Along the way he lived large and well. He mixed a penchant for cards, ponies, and quite a few women into a high-rolling life style. He left behind six children, aged 7 to 42, by three wives and a long-term lover, British actress Sally Adams, mother of Nicollette Sheridan. He had one child with Adams, son Nicholas (the on-again-off-again boyfriend of *90210*'s Tori Spelling). Though Sheridan had taken his name when Savalas lived with her mother, she later said, "He left my life very abruptly. And as far as I am concerned, he's out of my life for good." In 1980, Adams filed a $5-million palimony suit against the actor, eventually settling for a reported $1 million.

With his third and last wife, Julie Hovland, a former travel agent, Savalas remained Kojak to the end: a smart, gruff man who inspired loyalty and love. NO ONE CAN ENTER WITHOUT PERMISSION FROM THE KING, read a sign on his sickbed door at the Sheraton-Universal Hotel in Universal City, where he lived. Savalas, said his brother Teddy, "took all of life's detours. He packed so much in, he lived more like 210 years."

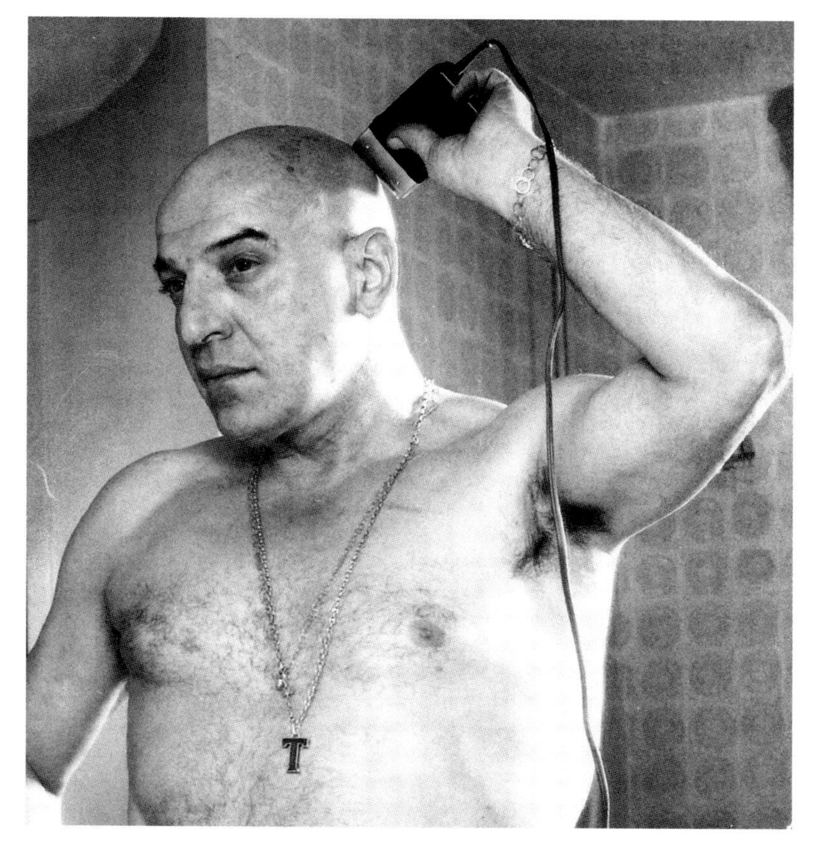

"My career," said Savalas (at left on the Kojak *set and tending his famous pate, right), "catapulted with my lack of hair."*

Henry Morgan

With a bow tie and barbed wit, often directed at the sponsors of his shows, sardonic humorist Henry Morgan, 79, was a favorite performer of radio audiences in the 1940s. For a while, he had his own show (that's the bespectacled Arnold Stang with him at left). In later years, Morgan, who died of lung cancer at his home in New York City, was a popular figure (along with Jayne Meadows, Bill Cullen and host Garry Moore) on CBS's TV hit, *I've Got A Secret*. Though blacklisted for a period, he came back to tickle the public fancy on such shows as *That Was the Week That Was* and *My World and Welcome to It*.

John Curry

Elegant figure skater John Curry, who won a gold medal at the 1976 Innsbruck Olympics, was often called Nureyev on Ice. The Birmingham, England, native became known as and is widely credited with making skating into an art form as well as a sport. Prevented by his factory-owner father from studying ballet as a child, Curry nonetheless added dance to his skating routines. "He brought the purist form of ballet to the ice," said fellow gold-medalist Peggy Fleming.

As a professional, Curry toured with his acclaimed "IceDancing" show in the '70s, and avoided the usual fate of ex-Olympians. "I never could see the point of spending 12 years training to go dress up in a Bugs Bunny suit," he once said. After he developed AIDS in 1991, Curry, who lived with his widowed mother Rita, let it be known that he was gay. He died of an AIDS-related heart attack at 44.

JESSICA TANDY

She was a phenomenon of grace and professionalism whose remarkable range over 67 years encompassed Shakespeare, Hitchcock (*The Birds*) and Tennessee Williams (above, as Blanche DuBois with Marlon Brando and Kim Hunter in 1947's *A Streetcar Named Desire*). By the time she died at 85 of ovarian cancer, she had won three Tonys and in 1989 became the oldest Oscar winner for *Driving Miss Daisy*. Critic Frank Rich wrote that Tandy was so "right and pure" that "only poets, and not theater critics, should be allowed to write about her."

Encouraged by her working-class London family to act, she became a regular stage performer. In 1932 she married actor Jack Hawkins. They had a daughter, Susan, but the marriage didn't last. In 1940, Tandy came to America and met her husband of 52 years, actor Hume Cronyn, beginning the famous collaboration that included such movies as 1985's *Cocoon* and the 1977 Broadway hit *The Gin Game*. At first, though, Tandy received only bit parts and divided time raising Susan and her children with Cronyn—Christopher, 51, and Tandy, 48, an actress. But as Jessica got older she got busier—and toiled at the end through the growing pain of cancer. Explaining her stoicism, she said, "What makes life worth living is the work." For her it was always a class effort. "In this day, when actresses do stupid infomercials and everyone is such a phony, Jessica was just herself," says *Driving Miss Daisy* author Alfred Uhry. "She seemed totally true to everything she did."

GOODBYES 1994

French photographer *Robert Doisneau*, 81, noted for his images of Parisian street life, including the controversial "The Kiss at City Hall"; of complications following heart surgery.

Emmy-winning filmmaker *Marlon Riggs*, 37, condemned for his publicly-funded 1989 documentary about gay black men, *Tongues Untied*; of AIDS.

Serial-killer *John Wayne Gacy*, 52, convicted of murdering 33 young men and boys during the 1970s; put to death after 14 years of appeals by lethal injection at Illinois' Stateville prison.

Mexican-born *Gilbert Roland*, who portrayed the Cisco Kid in 11 films and appeared in some 90 others, including *Camille* and *The Bad and the Beautiful*; of prostate cancer at 88.

Psychoanalyst *Erik Erikson*, 91, prolific author and student of Sigmund Freud, known for his personality-development theory and coining the term "identity crisis"; of an infection.

Roy Plunkett, 83, who accidentally invented Teflon more than 50 years ago, thus spawning a multi-billion-dollar plastics industry; of cancer.

EUGÈNE IONESCO

One of the pillars of the Theater of the Absurd, the Romanian-born French playwright Eugène Ionesco, 84, used farce to explore themes of alienation and conformity. Between 1950 and 1980, Ionesco, who died of an undisclosed illness at his home in Paris, wrote 28 surrealistic plays, most notably *The Bald Soprano* (1950), *The Chairs* (1952) and *Rhinoceros* (1959).

BETTY FURNESS

Through three career changes and three husbands, Betty Furness, who died of stomach cancer at 78, had grit. "When you want something, don't take no for an answer," she once said. "And when rejection comes, don't take it personally." A teen-age fashion model, she hit the big screen (*Magnificent Obsession*, *Swing Time*) in the '30s, and by the '50s became one of TV's first pitchwomen, hawking Westinghouse refrigerators. After a stint as Lyndon Johnson's special assistant for consumer affairs in the '60s, Furness, who lived quietly in Hartsdale, N.Y., with her third husband (of 26 years), TV producer Leslie Midgley, headed the consumer-affairs agencies of New York State and New York City. In 1976 she became the crusading consumer reporter for *Today*. "She was my role model," says veteran anchor Jane Pauley. "There isn't anybody in television that I admired more."

TIP O'NEILL

He was the genially gruff embodiment of a 20th-century politician. With his bulbous nose, mane of white hair and large cigar, Thomas P. "Tip" O'Neill was an enduring symbol of the Democratic Party, who inspired trust and cooperation on both sides of the aisle. A rabid sports fan, O'Neill got his nickname from baseball player James Edward O'Neill, who had a knack of hitting foul tips. The politician hit few. When Tip died of a heart attack at 81, Senate Republican leader Bob Dole, one of the Boston liberal's staunchest critics, said, "He will go down in history as one of the great political leaders of our time."

Comfortable with power and a master of the deal, O'Neill became Speaker of the House in 1977, and presided with a steady hand during turbulent times. He was an early voice against the Vietnam war and a loud one favoring the impeachment of President Nixon. During the Reagan years, he called the Republican president "a cheerleader for selfishness." After retiring in 1987, O'Neill received $1 million to write his memoirs, *Man of the House*. He is survived by his wife Mildred, their five children and eight grandchildren. Fittingly, the Congressman's body lay in state in Boston's State House. After all, one of Tip's most enduring observations on the game he played so well was "All politics is local."

GOODBYES 1994

Beloved children's author and illustrator *Richard Scarry*, 74, many of whose 250 titles in print featured his favorite character, the top-hatted Lowly Worm; of a heart attack at his Swiss home.

Florida abortion doctor *John Bayard Britton*, 69, shotgunned to death along with his volunteer escort outside his Pensacola clinic by a radical right-to-lifer.

When Atlanta-based humorist and syndicated columnist *Lewis Grizzard*, 47, the raffish, unreconstructed voice of the South, was told his chances were slim to survive his fourth open-heart surgery (he died of brain damage during the procedure), he quipped, "When's the next bus to Albuquerque?"

Frances Heflin, 71, sister of actor Van Heflin and for 25 years *All My Children*'s long-suffering Mona Tyler, mother of voracious serial monogamist Erica Kane; of cancer.

Anna Hauptmann, 95, who spent decades trying to clear her husband Bruno's name after his execution in 1936 for the kidnap-murder of Charles Lindbergh's infant son.

PETER CUSHING

British actor Peter Cushing, 81, found his niche as a spectral heavy. In a movie career that spanned four decades, he played in at least 20 horror movies, including *The Man in the Iron Mask* (1939), *The Curse of Frankenstein* (1957) and such latter-day howlers as *The Satanic Rites of Dracula* (1978). Cushing, who died of cancer in Canterbury, England, may be best remembered as he is pictured here, for his portrayal of the evil commander Grand Moff Tarkin in *Star Wars*.

RALPH ELLISON

Ralph Ellison published just one novel in his lifetime. But he was no minor author. His seminal 1952 tale, *Invisible Man*, is the introspective, eloquent story of an anonymous black man who travels from the segregated South to New York City, where he lives in embittered obscurity. The book, called a "brilliant individual victory" by Nobel Prize winner Saul Bellow, has been translated into 17 languages. When Oklahoma-born Ellison, 80, died of pancreatic cancer, cared for by Fanny, his wife of 47 years, he was revered as a gentle man of American letters. A library job while he attended Alabama's Tuskegee Institute introduced him to the works of Twain, Faulkner and Melville. He quit school in 1936 to move to New York City and write short stories. After serving in the Merchant Marine during World War II, Ellison spent seven years creating *Invisible Man*, traveling each day to an office incongruously located at the back of a jewelry store on Fifth Avenue. Though Ellison inspired many African-American writers, he was criticized by black nationalists for his belief that great literature has no racial identity. "You don't write out of your skin, for God's sake," he said. "You write out of your imagination."

MARTHA RAYE

Milton Berle once called Martha Raye "one of the funniest women in the world." She may also have been one of the unhappiest. Indeed, Raye, who died at 78 of circulatory problems, led a life so riven by personal disaster that it became a classic cautionary tale of show business. A child vaudevillian, by the age of 20 she was cast alongside Bing Crosby in the 1936 film *Rhythm on the Range*. Her generous mouth, hearty voice and showgirl legs made her ideal for such musicals as 1937's *Artists and Models* and 1944's *Pinup Girl*. "They tried to make a glamor girl out of me," she later complained. "That was ridiculous. I was no glamor girl; I was a comedian."

Still, her career soared. She was a big hit on TV and with American GIs on USO tours (that's North Africa, above, in 1943). Her personal life, though, was a mess. Raye's most consistent relationship was with her agent, Nick Condos, whom she married twice and who fathered her only child, Melodye, now 50. None of her six other marriages lasted more than three years. Along the way, she became the TV spokesperson for Polident in the '80s, and had salted away an estimated $2.4 million. She married Mark Harris, an ex-hairdresser from Brooklyn, in 1991. He was 42; she was confined by a stroke to a wheelchair. Melodye petitioned the court to take control of her mother's estate from Harris, but the request was denied. She is accorded $1 in Raye's will; the balance goes to Harris. Last year Raye's health problems grew worse, and her left leg was amputated below the knee. Still, she seemed to take comfort in her last years with Harris. "He makes me feel young and womanly," she once said. "I'm really in love this time."

GOODBYES 1994

Pennsylvania's Republican Senator *Hugh Scott*, 93, who served in Congress for 34 years and was Senate Minority Leader during the Watergate era; of cardiac arrest.

Michael Peters, Emmy- and Tony Award-winning Broadway choreographer who staged Michael Jackson's "Beat It" and "Thriller" videos; of AIDS at 46.

Puckish and irreverent Italian fashion designer *Franco Moschino*, 44, who created such outrageously audacious outfits as a ball gown made of plastic garbage bags; of an intestinal tumor.

Colombia's World Cup soccer player, *Andrés Escobar*, 27, whose error of inadvertently deflecting the ball into his own net became a national cause of sorrow and blame. He was later shot and killed in Medellín by a gunman who may have been hired by a drug cartel.

Husky-voiced character actor *Robert Lansing*, 66, whose career began on Broadway in 1951 with *Stalag 17* and spanned such TV series as *Twelve O'Clock High*; of cancer.

Dr. Rollo May, 85, founder of the humanistic psychology movement in the 1960s, best known for his 1969 book, *Love and Will*; of congestive heart failure.

Jule Styne

Broadway composer Jule Styne, 88, who died in New York City of heart failure, wrote more than 1,500 songs in his long career. He was a piano prodigy who made his debut with the Chicago Symphony at the age of eight. Often working with his pal, lyricist Sammy Cahn (seen here), Styne wrote scores for such musicals as *Gypsy* and *Funny Girl*. He was also the man behind cabaret classics like "Diamonds Are a Girl's Best Friend" and the Barbra Streisand perennial, "People."

Dick Sargent

Few gay celebrities ever emerged from the closet quite as dramatically as Dick Sargent. From 1969 to 1972 the actor became "the second Darrin," replacing Dick York as Elizabeth Montgomery's husband on the ABC sitcom *Bewitched*. Realizing that revealing his homosexuality could wreck his career, he posed with buxom actresses and even added a phony failed marriage to his publicity bio.

But Sargent, who died of prostate cancer at 64, was incensed by California's failure to enact a gay-rights bill three years ago and became active in the cause. After he declared his sexuality at a National Coming Out Day event, he joked, "Now I'm a retroactive role model." He was more than that for co-star Montgomery. "He was a great friend," said the actress. "I will miss his love, his sense of humor and his courage."

JOHN CANDY

He seemed to pop up, larger than life, in nearly every other movie made during the past 10 years. But neither his supportive family nor his growing success could save John Candy from the dangers of obesity. Shortly after shooting his final scene in the Western comedy *Wagons East*, the 43-year-old Canadian-born actor, who carried some 330 lbs. on his 6' 3" frame, died of a heart attack. "He was a gentle, almost delicate man," says friend and fellow comic Harold Ramis."In that big body, it was ironic."

Indeed, Candy's size set him apart in a career that spanned two decades and nearly 40 feature films, including *The Blues Brothers*, *Uncle Buck* and *Cool Runnings*. He drew rave notices for his comic turn in *Splash*. "He doesn't add weight," wrote *New Yorker* critic Pauline Kael of his screen personae. "He adds bounce and imagination." A graduate of the Emmy-winning *SCTV* comedy series, he once said, "I went from macaroni and cheese to macaroni and lobster." Although dieting sometimes took off pounds, Candy never achieved permanent weight loss. His appetites caused him considerable pain. "I'm the one who has to look in the mirror," he once remarked, "and after a while it begins to eat at you."

Despite occasional diets and bouts of exercise, Candy changed little over the years, inside or out. He married his high school sweetheart, Rosemary, 44, a potter, in 1979 and bought a farm north of Toronto, where they raised their two children, Jennifer, 14, and Christopher, 9. He was extremely protective of his privacy in the brief periods he was off-screen. Said pal Carl Reiner, who directed him in *Summer Rental*: "If you look at the work he did, it was two lifetimes worth. It's almost as if he knew something might happen."

GOODBYES 1994

Journalist *William L. Shirer*, 89, World War II CBS European radio correspondent and author of *The Rise and Fall of the Third Reich* (1960); of heart ailments.

Dixy Lee Ray, 79, former chairwoman of the U.S. Atomic Energy Commission and governor of Washington; of a bronchial condition.

Former IBM Chairman *Thomas J. Watson Jr.*, 79, dubbed "the greatest capitalist who ever lived" by FORTUNE; of stroke complications.

Harvey Haddix, 68, former big-league pitcher with the Pirates and Cardinals who pitched 12 straight innings of perfect baseball in 1959; of emphysema.

Green Acres actor and Gene Autry's funny-voiced singing sidekick *Pat Buttram*, 78; of kidney failure.

John Bradley, 70, the last survivor of the six American servicemen who raised the U.S. flag on Iwo Jima in 1945; of a stroke.

Northern Exposure's orphaned moose *Morty*, 6; of an illness linked to cobalt and copper mineral deficiencies.

RICHARD NIXON

Before his death following a stroke at 81, Richard Nixon, the only U.S. President to be driven from office, was a man of many crises, and many lives. He made enemies—and a fair share of history. Long derided as "Tricky Dick," Nixon was a master of transformations. The crusading anti-Communist of the 1950s became the first President to reach out to China. The paranoid, vindictive villain of Watergate became the Sage of Saddle River, New Jersey.

Ambitious but painfully awkward socially, he was the second of five sons of Francis Nixon, a California lemon farmer, and Hannah Milhous, a pious Quaker. After earning a law degree at Duke University, Nixon married Patricia Ryan, a schoolteacher, and doted on daughters Tricia and Julie. "The best decision I ever made was choosing Pat to be my wife," he later said. (She died in 1993.)

His service in Congress gave him a crusader's credentials that helped bring him the GOP nomination as Dwight Eisenhower's running mate in 1952. After narrowly losing the 1960 presidential race to the telegenic John F. Kennedy, then losing the 1962 governor's race in California, Nixon was declared politically dead. Yet he managed a stunning comeback in 1968 by repackaging himself and promising to end the Vietnam War. Though his presidency was ultimately shattered by his clumsy efforts to cover up the Watergate burglary (an attempt to obtain material to damage the Democrats), he maintained his drive out of office, adopting an image as an independent and respected éminence grise, and publishing books on global affairs. "What can be done with willpower, he will do," said Henry Kissinger, his former Secretary of State. In the end, though, old age was the one opponent Nixon could not outsmart or simply outlast.

Resigning the Presidency in 1974 (left), Nixon was supported by a devastated Pat. The then-Vice President earned points by standing up to Soviet premier Nikita Khrushchev in Moscow in 1959.

DANITRA VANCE

The first black woman to join the cast of *Saturday Night Live*, comedian and actress Danitra Vance, 35, died of breast cancer in Markham, Illinois. She stayed with *SNL* only for the 1985 season before she returned to her first love, the theater. After her cancer was diagnosed in 1990 and she had a breast removed, she created a solo performance skit, *The Radical Girl's Guide to Radical Mastectomy*, which ran for a season off-Broadway.

HARRY NILSSON

Possessing a dry wit and an offbeat imagination, Brooklyn-born composer and singer Harry Nilsson was best known for "Everybody's Talkin' ," his Grammy Award-winning theme for 1969's *Midnight Cowboy*. Although his own albums met with modest success before his untimely death of a heart attack at 52, his songs, including "10 Little Indians" and "Cuddle Toy," were covered by such diverse talents as the Yardbirds and Herb Alpert. John Lennon called Nilsson his favorite American singer. The ex-Beatle produced his 1974 *Pussycats* album. Ringo Starr collaborated with Nilsson on the 1974 soundtrack of the movie *Son of Dracula*. By the '80s, he had mostly retired from writing to pursue business interests, including a film distribution company in Studio City, California.

George Peppard

His smooth good looks seemed sun-baked and yet somehow unexceptional, and so did his résumé: A promising movie actor in the '60s (*Breakfast at Tiffany's*, *The Carpetbaggers*), he went on to become a TV star in the '70s and '80s. George Peppard portrayed the wealthy, high-living Boston investigator *Banacek*, and switched images to play tough, cigar-chewing Col. Hannibal Smith in NBC's *The A-Team*.

But until his death of pneumonia at 65, Peppard had a bumpy ride during a 40-year career no one would envy. He was a hard drinker until he gave up booze in 1978. "When I drank, I was my own worst enemy." He was also a hard case as a husband. He took six wives, and two of them were Elizabeth Ashley. In her memoirs, Ashley claims that Peppard once tried to hit her with a frying pan. "Mine isn't a string of victories," he once told his friend *New York Post* columnist Cindy Adams. "It's no golden past. I'm no George Peppard fan."

Yet many others were. "If George said he would stand by you, you knew he would," says his friend, actor Pat Hingle. "There aren't many in Hollywood you can say that about." Adds actor Rip Torn, who studied at Lee Strasberg's famed Actor's Studio with Peppard, "He had a wonderful, ironic sense of humor." Still, George Hamilton, who made two films with Peppard (*Home from the Hill*; *The Victors*), remembers him as "weighted down by a sort of inner sadness I could never really fathom."

GOODBYES 1994

Allan G. Odell, 90, creator of the fabled Burma-Shave roadside advertising signs; of natural causes. A typical Odell rhyme: "Every/Sheba/Wants a Sheik/Strong of Muscle/Smooth of Cheek/Burma Shave."

Cable TV pioneer and creator of the TelePrompTer *Irving B. Kahn*, 76; of a heart attack.

Veteran character actor *Claude Akins*, 67, best known as Sheriff Lobo on *B.J. and the Bear* and for his Aamco transmission ads; of stomach cancer.

William Levitt, real estate developer whose some 17,000 tract houses on Long Island, N.Y. set the postwar style for affordable suburban housing; of kidney failure at 86.

Champion downhill skier *Ulrike Maier*, 29, star of the Austrian World Cup team and mother of a four-year-old daughter; of a broken neck sustained in a 60-mph fall during a race.

Character actor *Hal Smith*, best remembered as town drunk Otis Campbell on *The Andy Griffith Show*; in his sleep at 77.

Sorrell Booke, 64, the Yale School of Drama graduate who played "Boss" Hogg on *The Dukes of Hazzard*; of cancer.

“Papa” John Creach

Electric violinist John Creach, 76, a classically trained musician, got his nickname of “Papa” as a revered golden oldie, both playing and singing, with the San Francisco psychedelic rock group Jefferson Airplane in the early ’70s. The Beaver Falls, Pennsylvania, native, who died of heart and respiratory complications at a Los Angeles hospital, also performed with Airplane’s spinoff group, Hot Tuna, from 1971 to ’73.

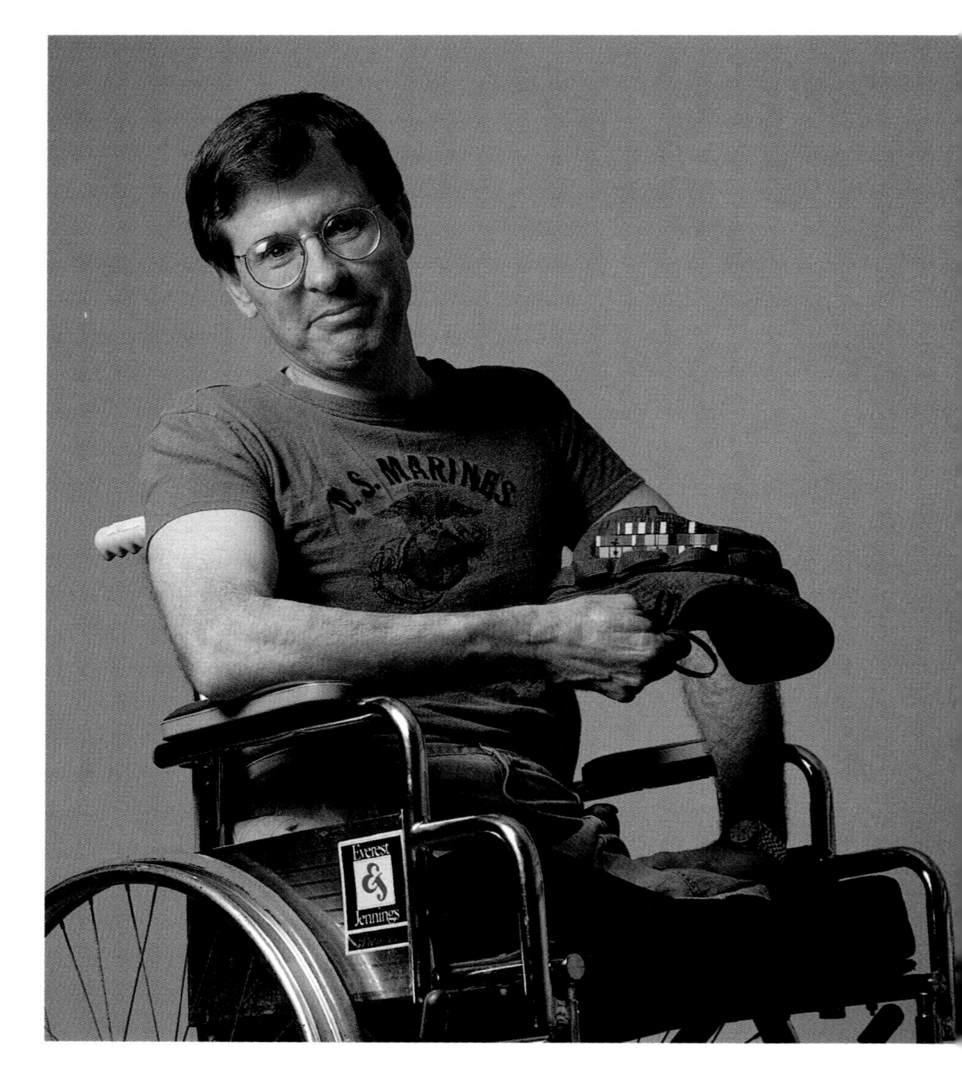

Lewis Puller Jr.

The only son of Gen. Lewis “Chesty” Puller Sr., whose World War II and Korea exploits made him the most decorated Marine officer in history, Lewis Puller himself became a Marine hero who inspired fellow Vietnam vets with his 1991 Pulitzer Prize-winning autobiography, *Fortunate Son*.

In that volume, Puller, who had lost his legs and parts of both hands in action in 1968, chronicled his recovery from his injuries and his bouts with depression and alcoholism. He was married for 26 years to Linda “Toddy” Puller, a member of the Virginia House of Delegates. But recently, he had fallen back into pain and depression, causing Puller, at age 48, to kill himself by means of a self-inflicted gunshot wound.

MELINA MERCOURI

"I thought it was death I was afraid of," Melina Mercouri recently mused. "But now I know my worst fear is that I should no longer be loved." Her fear was groundless. When the news reached Athens that the beloved embodiment of Greek passion had died at 68 of lung cancer, flags dropped to half-mast, theaters closed, and radio and TV stations played Mercouri—her husky-throated cabaret songs and clips from her signature 1960 film, *Never on Sunday*.

The daughter of a Minister of the Interior, she defied her parents at 17 by marrying a wealthy Greek merchant much older than she (they divorced in 1962) and enrolling in the National Theatre of Greece. After triumphing onstage in Athens and Paris, she became an international star as a fiercely independent Piraeus prostitute in *Sunday*, appearing opposite her then-lover, Jules Dassin, whom she married in 1966. (He was with her when she died.)

But Mercouri chose to devote most of her ardor to politics. When she spoke out against the military dictatorship that ruled Greece from 1967 to 1974, she was stripped of her citizenship. She returned to Greece in 1974 after the election of the New Democracy Party and herself served as a Member of Parliament from Piraeus from 1977 to 1989, as Culture Minister from '81 to '89, and as a founder of the Panhellenic Socialist Movement. "I thought she was the happiest she'd ever been, while in politics," said her friend of 30 years, costume designer Theoni Aldredge. "Melina was beautiful and flamboyant, and everything she did was to the utmost."

GOODBYES 1994

British film director *Lindsay Anderson*, 71, who won an Oscar for 1954's *Thursday's Children*, a groundbreaking documentary about the deaf; of a heart attack.

Former actress *Sara Taylor*, 99, mother of Elizabeth Taylor; of natural causes.

James Aubrey Jr., 75, blunt CBS executive known as the "Smiling Cobra," who brought *The Beverly Hillbillies*, *The Dick Van Dyke Show* and *Green Acres* to television; of a heart attack.

Roswell Gilbert, whose 1985 shooting of his ailing wife ignited the national debate on mercy killing; in his sleep at 85. Gilbert was granted clemency in 1990, after 5 1/2 years in prison.

Former Stockbridge, Mass., police chief *William Obanhein*, 69, immortalized as Officer Obie in Arlo Guthrie's '60s anthem "Alice's Restaurant"; of heart disease.

Actor *Jack Dodson*, familiar fixture as county clerk Howard Sprague on *The Andy Griffith Show* and *Mayberry R.F.D.*; of heart failure at 63.

JAMES CLAVELL

He said he was "just a storyteller." But James Clavell, who died of cancer at 69, penned tales (including *Tai-Pan* and *Noble House*) that stuck on the bestseller lists for years. When his 1,207-page *Shogun* was televised in 1980, it was the most-watched miniseries after *Roots*. Clavell lived at homes in Switzerland and France with his wife, actress April Stride, and their daughters Michaela and Holly. He is shown (left) in Hong Kong doing literary reconnaissance.

WALTER LANTZ

Walter Lantz, 94, was already a successful, self-employed animator in 1941 when he and his wife, Grace, got the idea for the cartoon character that made his scrawled signature on the nation's movie screens a part of American popular culture. Woody Woodpecker—the off-key, off-base, off-the-wall bird who careened through dozens of animations—was the basis of a multimillion-dollar cartoon empire that also included Oswald the Rabbit and Andy Panda. Woody's voice and his hysterical trademark laugh were supplied over the decades by two people: the legendary Mel Blanc and, later, by Grace Lantz herself. Woody was a labor of love. Walter, who died of heart disease at a Los Angeles hospital, and Grace based their bird on an obnoxious woodpecker that disrupted their California honeymoon. That's all, folks.

PEDRO ZAMORA

HIV, and positive, Pedro Zamora of MTV's *Real World* lived his too-brief life to its limit. For many in his generation, the Cuban-born Zamora—just 22 at his death—put a human and unforgettable face on AIDS. Each week on *The Real World*, the documentary series in which groups of young men and women become real-life roommates for four months, viewers (and Zamora's six MTV roomies) watched with apprehension, then admiration, as he fell in love with AIDS activist Sean Sasser; spent hours in an emergency room; made peace with the one roommate (Rachel) who'd been wary of him; and continued his years-long campaign for education—calmly but forcefully telling high school and college students what life was like with HIV.

Zamora, with part of his family, escaped Cuba in the 1980 Mariel boat lift, at age 8. By 13, the transplanted Miami teen realized he was gay and began to cruise the bars. He was diagnosed with HIV four years later. Through the support of Body Positive, a Miami-based AIDS organization, he began to lecture on the dangers of unprotected sex. His good friend Alex Escarano says Zamora, a high school honor student, was messianic about his AIDS work: "He wanted to reach people." At the end, Zamora was too ill to know that one dream had come true: His family, scattered for 14 years between the U.S. and Cuba, had reunited—if only to say goodbye to the son and brother who had become a symbol of a global tragedy.

GOODBYES 1994

Dancer-choreographer *Erick Hawkins*, 85, central modern dance figure and onetime husband of the late Martha Graham; of prostate cancer.

Actor *Dedrick Gobert*, 22, who had supporting roles in *Boyz N the Hood* and *Poetic Justice*; shot to death in a fight during an illegal drag race.

Yippie-turned-Yuppie *Jerry Rubin*, 56, member of the Chicago Seven; of cardiac arrest following massive injuries incurred when he was hit by a car.

Jeffrey Dahmer, 34, sentenced to 936 years in prison for the murders and dismemberment of 16 young men; beaten to death at Columbia Correctional Institution in Wisconsin.

William Leonard, former head of CBS News who helped oversee the creation of *60 Minutes* back in 1968; of a stroke at 68.

Fred Smith, known as Sonic, the guitarist for the '60s rock band MC5 and husband of punk rocker Patti Smith; of a heart attack at 45.

Bandleader *Milton "Shorty" Rogers*, 70, jazz trumpeter and arranger who helped pioneer the mid-1950s style known as West Coast jazz; of liver failure.

Smoky-voiced jazz vocalist *Carmen McRae*, 74, one of America's finest song stylists and a skilled scat singer; of complications from a stroke.

BURT LANCASTER

During his heyday, it seemed there was never a pair of shoulders so broad, a set of teeth so white or a laugh of such bighearted, roof-raising menace. Those elements conspired to form the archetypal Tough Guy, who ruled the terrain around him—be it rifle company or circus ring, pirate ship or preacher's pulpit—by the sheer power of his personality. Says his friend, actor Ed Asner, of that screen persona: "He was the rottenest son of a bitch in the world, carrying those big ivories—but you just knew you couldn't hate him."

Therein lay the essence of the rich—and sometimes risky—characters that Burt Lancaster chose to play in a career that started late (at 33, in 1946's *The Killers*) and roared through some 80 films for screen and TV, bringing him an Oscar for 1960's *Elmer Gantry* and fame as one of the last of the classic Hollywood stars. But sometimes on screen, and in his very private life as well, there was a genuine sentimental side to Lancaster, 80, who died of a heart attack in Los Angeles with his wife, Susie, at his side. "I loved his soft, gentle nature," Susie says. "There was an unspoken language between us, transmitted by a touch or a glance." Lancaster was twice divorced and the father of five when he married the former Susie Martin in 1990. Shortly after, he was partially paralyzed by a stroke and spent his last years in a wheelchair.

His upbringing in New York City's East Harlem, with his postal-clerk father, hardly prepared Lancaster for gentleness. He was a high school basketball star and went to New York University for two years before improbably running off to join a circus high-wire act. Drafted in 1942, he shifted to stage work, producing shows across Europe and North Africa for the Army. After the war, he moved to Hollywood and compiled his tough-guy résumé. He also went out on a limb to play against type. He portrayed an alcoholic chiropractor in 1952's *Come Back, Little Sheba*; a fool of a lover in 1955's *The Rose Tattoo*; and a savage Broadway gossip columnist in 1957's *Sweet Smell of Success*. "I'd still be the same punk kid I used to be back in East Harlem," he told a reporter, "if I was afraid to take a chance."

Lancaster's risk-taking was strictly professional. He was quiet and paternal at home, not unlike his friend, Kirk Douglas. The two battled their way through a string of movies, most notably *Gunfight at the OK Corral* and *Seven Days in May*. "Kirk would be the first to admit he's difficult to work with," Lancaster once said, ``and I'd be the second." The grieving Douglas issued only a simple statement upon his friend's death. "Burt isn't really dead," it read in part. "People years from now will still be seeing us shooting at each other."

Whether a smiling swashbuckler, as in The Crimson Pirate *(left), or a priapic G.I. with Deborah Kerr in* From Here to Eternity, *Lancaster always left 'em panting for more.*

BARRY SULLIVAN

One of Hollywood's best journeyman character actors, rugged-looking Barry Sullivan, who died of a respiratory ailment at 81, worked on the stage, in films and on television in a career that spanned some four decades. The native New Yorker made his Broadway debut in 1936 and went on to Hollywood in such films as *Lady in the Dark* (1944), *The Bad and the Beautiful* (1953) and *Tell Them Willie Boy Is Here* (1969). During TV's golden age, he did turns on *Bonanza* and *Cannon*, and was a regular on the series *Harbourmaster, The Tall Man* and *The Road West*.

VITAS GERULAITIS

Before Andre Agassi, the image-is-everything kid, there was leonine Vitas Gerulaitis, the tennis world's original flamboyant. He drove a yellow Rolls-Royce, partied at Studio 54 and dated actresses. The Brooklyn-born Lithuanian-American was never a superstar player (though he ranked 3rd in 1978), but he was the sport's number one personality in the days of such ego-trippers as pal John McEnroe. In 1983, however, the good times were interrupted when Vitas was named by a grand jury in a conspiracy to buy cocaine. He was never indicted, but his image was tarnished. Over the past few years, he had undergone treatment for drug abuse and seemed to be back on track. At age 40, he had begun a promising career as a TV analyst with ESPN and CBS. When his body was found at a cottage on the Long Island estate of a friend, his inner circle feared that he had succumbed to drugs again. But Gerulaitis was killed by carbon monoxide poisoning. The colorless, ordorless and lethal gas, which causes some 5,000 deaths per year in the U.S., apparently leaked into the cottage's air-conditioning system.

HARRIET NELSON

She was a singer when she joined the big band of Ozzie Nelson in 1932. But by the time she died of congestive heart failure at 85, Harriet Nelson was much more: She embodied the wise, trustworthy image of what America wanted in motherhood. Her life was filled with love and devotion, considering that it was put on such public display. Beginning in 1944, *The Adventures of Ozzie and Harriet* ran for a decade on radio and 14 years on television, making Ozzie, Harriet and their sons David and Ricky the most visible touchstones of American family life as it was imagined, with wondrous simplicity, in mid-20th century. "The show was family," Harriet said in a rare interview three years ago. "We worked every day of the week, and we loved it."

Now only David, a TV producer, remains. Ozzie died of cancer in 1975 at age 68, and Rick perished at 45 in a 1985 plane crash. Grandma Harriet doted on Rick's kids, daughter Tracy and twin sons Matthew and Gunnar, who have carried on the family tradition. Tracy appears on *Melrose Place*, and the twins emulate their rock-star father. "She had a wonderful sense of humor," Tracy recalls. "I once asked her, 'What do I say to people who ask me what advice you've given me about show business?' She said, 'That I told you to take your makeup off before you go to bed.' "

GOODBYES 1994

Dub Taylor, character actor who appeared in more than 300 movies, including memorable turns in *Bonnie and Clyde*, *The Wild Bunch* and *Back to the Future II*; of congestive heart failure at 87.

Faith Davis, 95, listed in *The Guinness Book of Records* as part of the oldest set of triplets in the world; of natural causes.

Actress and onetime Ziegfeld Follies star dancer *Lina Basquette*, 87, who was married nine times to seven different husbands, including Jack Dempsey and Nelson Eddy, and who launched a new career in 1947 as a breeder of Great Danes; of lymphoma.

Fred Lebow, 62, creator and tireless promoter of the New York City Marathon; of brain cancer. Lebow's condition was diagnosed in 1990, yet he courageously finished the 26-mile-plus race in 1992.

Kristen Pfaff, 27, bassist for Courtney Love's band, Hole; of a heroin overdose just four months after Love's husband and heroin addict Kurt Cobain committed suicide.

JOSEPH COTTEN

He always sounded like he had a mild cold, but for over four decades, that nasal voice graced nearly 60 films. Actor Joseph Cotten, 88, who got his big break on Orson Welles's Mercury Theater on the radio, went on to appear in Welles's movies *Citizen Kane*, *The Magnificent Ambersons* and *Journey into Fear*. He starred as well in such classics as *Gaslight*, *The Third Man* and the horror cult hit, *Hush...Hush, Sweet Charlotte*. When he died of pneumonia at his L.A. home, actress Patricia Medina, 73, his wife of 33 years, was at his side.

CHRISTY HENRICH

At age 22, champion gymnast Christy Henrich finally lost the battle with anorexia nervosa and bulimia that plagued her brief career and life. The sport, says Olympic medalist Cathy Rigby, who once suffered from the disorder, "is fertile ground for anorexia." At that world-class level, the average size among women contenders is 4' 9", 88 lbs. Henrich, who stood 4' 10", had a compulsive fear of being too heavy, and when the Independence, Missouri, teenager failed to qualify for the U.S. Olympic team in 1988, she became convinced it was because of her weight. Despite the help and support of psychologists, physicians, her parents and Bo Moreno, her fiancé of four years, Henrich was frequently hospitalized (at one point she weighed a mere 47 lbs.) and drained of the strength to compete. Last year, with Moreno's devoted attention, she rallied, began to eat and gained 20 lbs. in one month. But she had, said doctors, passed the point of no return, and suffered a general physical breakdown. When she died of multiple organ system failure in a Kansas City hospital, she weighed only 60 lbs.

DACK RAMBO

"The streets of heaven are too crowded with angels. . . . They number a thousand for every red ribbon worn tonight," said Tom Hanks when he accepted the Oscar for his performance as a lawyer dying of AIDS in *Philadelphia*. Several hours before the ceremony, one more name was added to those ranks—though Dack Rambo, 53, hardly regarded himself as angelic. The actor died of complications of AIDS at his California ranch, with his mother, Beatrice, and sister, Beverly, at his side.

The intensely handsome Rambo, best known as J.R. Ewing's cousin Jack on CBS's *Dallas* and Congressman Grant Harrison on NBC's daytime soap *Another World*, remains perhaps the most familiar Hollywood face to go public with his HIV-positive status. "It feels like freedom," Rambo said of his September 1991 announcement. Thus unfettered, he was remarkably frank in interviews recounting dozens of unsafe sexual encounters, with both men and women, plus previous addictions to alcohol and tranquilizers.

Dack and his identical twin brother, Dirk—who died in a 1967 car crash—began their careers shortly after high school. Despite success, Dack worried about what he described as showbiz homophobia. Fearing his *Another World* castmates would turn chilly once they learned of his HIV status, he quit the soap—and his career. In the last years of his life, Rambo underwent chemotherapy for an AIDS-related cancer and also turned to holistic treatment. Last summer he claimed he'd halted the virus through prayer. "There is no disease that cannot be healed," he said then. "I will believe that until the day I drop."

GOODBYES 1994

Author *Christopher Lasch*, 61, who explored American mores in his best-seller *The Culture of Narcissism*; of cancer.

British filmmaker *Derek Jarman*, 52, known for his homosexually themed movies; of AIDS.

Gloria Hatrick Stewart, 75, wife of actor Jimmy Stewart for 45 years; of lung cancer.

Actor *Ezra Stone*, 76, best known for his Broadway and radio role as Henry Aldrich; in an automobile accident.

Randy Shilts, journalist and author of *And the Band Played On*; of complications from AIDS, at 42.

Actor *Fernando Rey*, 76, who played the narcotics merchant Charnier in *The French Connection*; of bladder cancer.

Hard-drinking poet *Charles Bukowski*, 73, who wrote the screenplay for *Barfly* as well as 32 volumes of poems; of leukemia.

Health columnist *Dr. Stuart Berger*, 40, author of *Dr. Berger's Immune Power Diet*; of a heart attack brought on by cocaine and obesity.

TV sitcom *We Got It Made* actor *Tom Villard*, 40; of AIDS.

Louis Nizer, 92, one of the century's leading celebrity lawyers and the author of 10 books, including his 1962 autobiography *My Life in Court*; of kidney failure.

Gravel-voiced acting veteran *Lionel Stander*, 86, who played the chauffeur Max on *Hart to Hart*; of lung cancer.

Elizabeth Glaser

Few have waged such a private battle on so public a stage as Elizabeth Glaser. HIV-positive herself from a 1981 blood transfusion, she co-founded the Pediatric AIDS Foundation. She and husband Paul Michael Glaser, 52, the *Starsky and Hutch* costar, had lost daughter Ariel (seen with Mom, Dad and brother Jake) to the disease at age 7 in 1988. (Jake, now 10, is also infected.) Glaser's dedication to children with the virus prodded Congress to fund research programs and galvanized A-listers like Jack Nicholson and Tom Cruise to dramatize the cause. After Glaser died at 47, her friend Cher said, "It was as if the disease brought out the best in her, brought her to her fullest potential."

Virginia Kelley

Flamboyant and passionate, she was the driving parental force behind the saxophone-playing Rhodes scholar who sits in the Oval Office. A thrice-widowed (and four times married) former anesthesiological nurse, Virginia Kelley, 70, who died of breast cancer in Hot Springs, Arkansas, gave her sons Bill and Roger Clinton a *joie de vivre* despite the family's hardscrabble life. A dedicated gambler and a major Elvis Presley fan, fond of striking red, white and blue outfits, Kelley spent her last weekend attending two Barbra Streisand concerts in Vegas. The singer donated $200,000 to establish a breast cancer research fund in her name. Another enduring legacy was her optimism. "Bill and his mother," Hillary Rodham Clinton once said, "always see the glass half full."

Henry Mancini

When choosing a title for his 1989 autobiography, Henry Mancini picked the question a movie songwriter might ask about the audience: *Did They Mention the Music?* In Mancini's case, of course, people always did—often while announcing his latest Academy Award nomination.

Mancini, 70, who died of cancer at his home in Bel Air with his wife Ginny by his side, earned 18 of those during his 40-year career, winning a Best Song Oscar for "Moon River" from *Breakfast at Tiffany's* (1961) and a Best Score Oscar for 1982's *Victor/Victoria*. He may be best remembered, though, for his Oscar-nominated hit, "The Pink Panther Theme" (1964), which graced the Peter Sellers movies and a syndicated television cartoon series.

The son of an Italian immigrant steelworker, Mancini grew up in Aliquippa, Pennsylvania. After World War II service in the Air Force and the infantry, he joined the Glenn Miller Orchestra in 1946 and fell in love with its singer, Ginny O'Connor, who was one of the original members of Mel Torme's Mel Tones. "They'd all file on the bus and leave the seat empty next to me," she reminisced recently, "and that would be the only place left for him to sit." The couple married in 1947 in Hollywood, where Mancini went to work writing music at Universal Studios. Over the next few decades, he churned out theme music for more than a dozen TV shows (*Peter Gunn* and *Remington Steele* among them), scored more than 80 films and collected 20 Grammys. "He was the greatest songwriter since Irving Berlin," says Andy Williams, whose "Moon River" recording sold millions of copies and became a signature theme. "And he was the nicest man I ever knew."

GOODBYES 1994

Angela Lakeberg, 11 months, the Siamese twin surgically separated from her sister Amy (who died during the operation); of cardiorespiratory complications.

Pulitzer-prize-winning journalist and TIME magazine drama critic *William A. Henry III*, author of *In Defense of Elitism* and a Jackie Gleason biography, *The Great One*; of a heart attack at 44.

Pioneer gospel singer *Marion Williams*, 66, who recorded 10 albums during her career and received a $274,000 genius fellowship from the MacArthur Foundation; of vascular complications from diabetes.

Actor *Cameron Mitchell*, 75, who over a 40-year career won critical praise for his performance as Happy in the original Broadway staging of *Death of a Salesman* in 1949, appeared in more than 90 films (*The Oxbow Incident, Carousel*) and played the hard-drinking Buck Cannon in NBC's *The High Chaparral*; of lung cancer at 75.

Earl Strong, 66, a flamboyant and fearless NBA referee for 33 years; of a cancerous brain tumor.

Tom Ewell

Originally a stage actor, Tom Ewell, who died at 85 after a long series of illnesses, made more than a dozen films, including *Adam's Rib* (1949). He most often portrayed inept woman-chasers and harried, ordinary guys. In that persona, he costarred with two of Hollywood's most luminous sex symbols: Jayne Mansfield in *The Girl Can't Help It* (1956) and, in the memorable scene at left, Marilyn Monroe in *The Seven Year Itch* (1955). In the mid-'70s, he became a regular on ABC's detective series, *Baretta*.

Macdonald Carey

A veteran screen star whose more than 50 films included *Dream Girl* and *Shadow of a Doubt*, Macdonald Carey, who died of cancer at 81, was better known for the past 29 years as Dr. Tom Horton, the wise paterfamilias of NBC's *Days of Our Lives*. "The show had millions of family members across the country," says *Days* alumnus Bill Hayes. "It's like we all lost a grandfather."

After the movie roles stopped coming, the Iowa-born Carey snapped up the soap part in 1965. "I was so happy to take it," he said, "with a wife [Betty Heckscher] and six kids to support." Despite success, a life-long love of the bottle finally caught up with Carey. Alcoholism strained his relationships with his children and his marriage. The Careys divorced in 1970. In 1982 Carey joined Alcoholics Anonymous and, bolstered by Lois Kraines, his companion for the last 22 years, never took another drink.

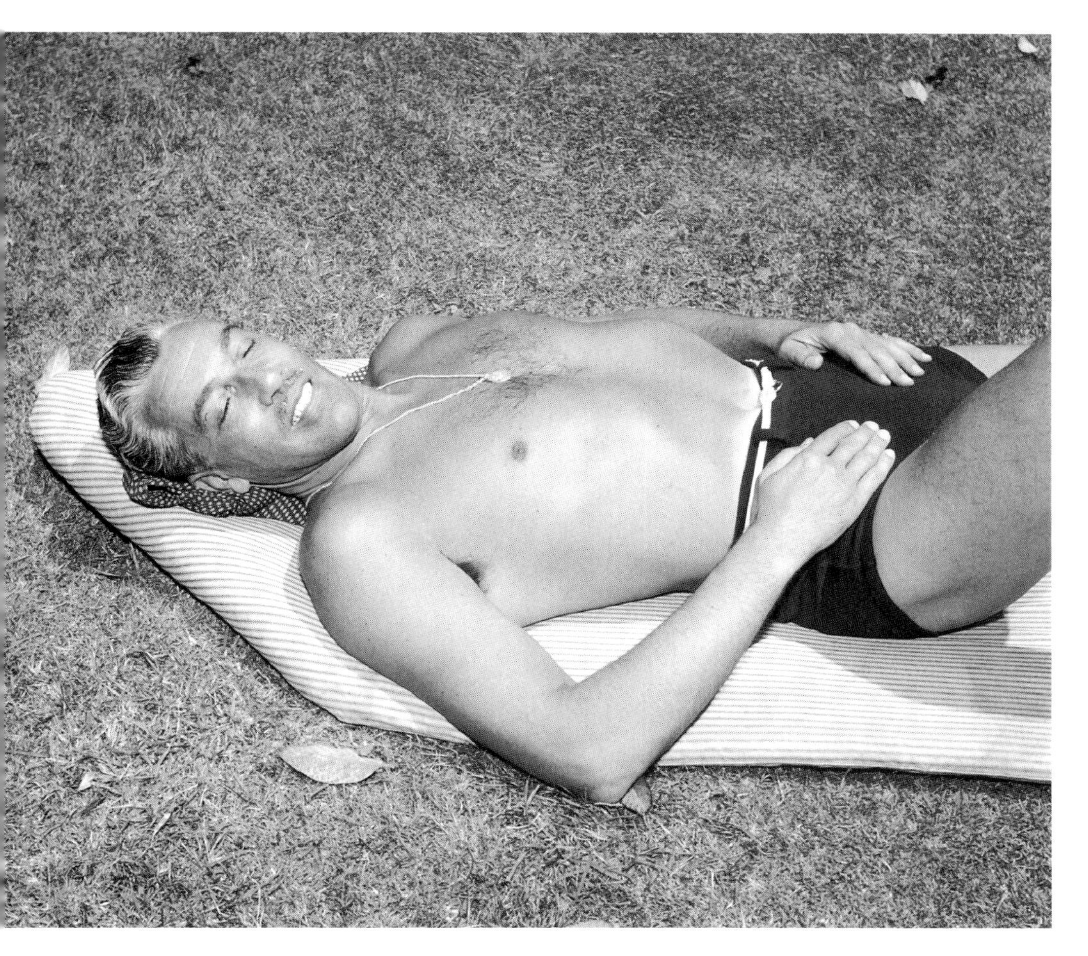

Cesar Romero

In the 1940s and '50s, Cesar Romero was one of Hollywood's most classically handsome leading men, who set hearts beating when on the screen and in steamy publicity shots (like that above). Yet in the role he may be best remembered for—the Joker, Batman's maniacal archenemy who stalked the cartoonish streets of Gotham in the campy '70s TV series—Romero had to hide his still-fabulous kisser beneath a thick layer of clownish greasepaint.

Romero, who died at 86 of a blood clot, didn't mind forsaking his looks for a juicy, career-reviving part. But he balked when the producers asked him to shave off his proudest feature: his mustache. Recalls *Batman* star Adam West: "It was as if he'd be losing all those wonderful movies he made [*The Gay Caballero*, *Captain from Castile*] when he was the dashing Latin Romeo. So the producers said, 'Okay, just dab some white makeup over it.' But if you look closely, you can see the mustache through the greasepaint."

In his heyday you could always glimpse the suave, debonair Romero (a self-described "Latin from Manhattan" whose parents were formerly wealthy Cuban émigrés) escorting the likes of Joan Crawford, Marlene Dietrich and Ann Sheridan around to the chic restaurants and watering holes of Beverly Hills and New York City. Romance, however, was never in the Joker's cards. "I have no regret," he once said of his un-altared status.

And yet in death, women couldn't seem to praise him enough. "He was so congenial. There wasn't a phony bone in his body," says his friend Dorothy Lamour. "He was elegant and eloquent," recalls another old pal, actress Anne Jeffreys. "He was," she reflects, "the last of an era."

GOODBYES 1994

Former pro golfer *Julius Boros*, 74, winner of the U.S. Open in 1952 and 1963; of a heart attack while sitting in a golf cart in Fort Lauderdale.

Baron Marcel Bich, 79, the former fountain pen salesman who created the Bic ballpoint pen in the early '50s.

Ezra Taft Benson, 94, the 13th head of the Mormon Church and Secretary of Agriculture in the Eisenhower Administration; of congestive heart failure.

Author *Dennis Potter*, best known for his pungent British TV dramas *The Singing Detective* and *Pennies from Heaven*; of pancreatic cancer at 59, not long after taping an unforgettable interview while nipping from a flask of morphine.

Merwyn Bogue, 86, better known as Ish Kabibble, a member of Kay Kyser's band from 1931 to 1951 and a regular on radio's *Kay Kyser's Kollege of Musical Knowledge*; of pulmonary disease.

Herbert Anderson, 77, *Dennis the Menace*'s owlish TV father, Henry Mitchell; in his sleep.

JACKIE

In death, as in life, she was the portrait of a lady. Beautiful until the end; so poised she was sending out thank-you notes from her deathbed; so thoughtful she planned a funeral that, once again, showed a nation how to mourn. And mourn we do, for when Jacqueline Lee Bouvier Kennedy Onassis died at 64, of a cancer that moved too swiftly, she may have been prepared, but we were not.

Certainly the image of a grieving Jackie standing with her children remains frozen in an awful moment that separates an American past that was too romanticized from a present that is too brutal. But three decades later, Jackie stood for so much more. We were not ready to give up our glimpses of her—elegant, impenetrable, but somehow more approachable as she aged—when she ventured out into book editing, the philanthropic and social whirl or onto a merry-go-round with her grandchildren. We were not ready to have that already poignant threesome— the Kennedy tableau of Jacqueline, Caroline and John Jr.—reduced now to two survivors going arm-in-arm into the future. And above all, we were not ready to let her leave without having our questions answered. Quite simply, how did she do it? How did the most famous woman in the world so gracefully endure the fickle winds of American affection? And what, behind those dark glasses and that mysterious smile, was she really thinking?

She once compared herself and Jack (at the White House during his Presidency) to "icebergs," whose real selves stayed hidden. This, she added, "was a bond between us."

Not so much raised as groomed, Jackie inherited traits from both her flamboyant stockbroker father, John "Black Jack" Bouvier, and perfectionist mother, Janet (above); before meeting JFK, she was briefly a newspaper "Inquiring Camera Girl" (left). Whether showing her children how to play, or how to behave with dignity, Jackie was a devoted mother.

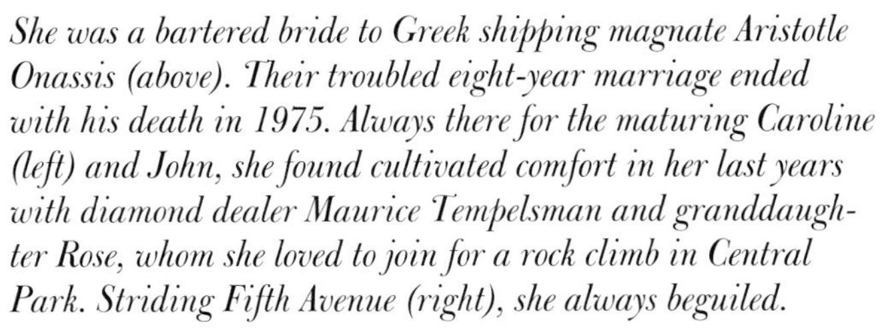

She was a bartered bride to Greek shipping magnate Aristotle Onassis (above). Their troubled eight-year marriage ended with his death in 1975. Always there for the maturing Caroline (left) and John, she found cultivated comfort in her last years with diamond dealer Maurice Tempelsman and granddaughter Rose, whom she loved to join for a rock climb in Central Park. Striding Fifth Avenue (right), she always beguiled.

PICTURE CREDITS

COVER Brian Quigley • **BACK COVER:** (clockwise from top) Davis Factor/Visages, Niviere/Sichov/Sipa Press, Pool/Globe Photos, Bonnie Schiffman/Onyx • **TITLE PAGE:** Steve Goldstein/Outline • **CONTENTS:** (top to bottom) Patrick Pagnano/CBS, Sygma, Diana Walker/Gamma Liaison, Miguel/Alpha/Globe, Ed Sirrs/Retna

MOMENTS TO REMEMBER 4 (top) Albert Ferreira/DMI, Agence France-Presse • 5 (both) Reuters/Bettmann • 6-7 Richard Hartog/The Outlook/Sipa • 8 (top) Neal Preston/Retna, Brian Rasic/Rex USA • 9 Chris Haston/NBC • 10 (top) Deborah Feingold/Styled by Jane Harrison, Robert Trippett/Sipa • 11 AP/Wide World • 12-13 Bruce Chambers/Orange County Register/Saba • 14 (top) Robert Trippett/Sipa, AP/Wide World • 15 (top) The White House, AP/Wide World • 16-17 Patrick Pagnano/CBS • 18-19 (clockwise from right) Jimi Stratton/LGI, Kelly Jordan/Sygma, Alan Berliner, AP/Wide World, AP/Wide World

HOT PROPERTIES 21 Andrew Brusso/Outline • 22 (top) Robert Beck, Mark Sennet/Onyx • 23 (left) © Walt Disney Pictures, Davis Factor/Visages • 24 (top to bottom) Mark Sennet/Onyx, Courtesy The Coca-Cola Company, Aaron Rapoport/Onyx • 25 (top) Bob Frame/LaMoine, Robin Bowman • 26 (top) Mark Sennet/Onyx, Camhi/Stills/Retna • 27 (top) Wayne Stambler/Sygma, Micheal McLaughlin • 28 (top to bottom) Ann States/Saba, Ruedi Hofman/Onyx, E.J. Camp/Outline • 29 (top) Bob Frame, Peter Nash • 30 (top) Robert Walker/Gamma Liaison, Steve Liss • 31 (top) George Holz/Onyx, Neal Preston/Retna • 32 (clockwise from top) Reynolds/Sygma, Steve Sands/Outline, Jeffrey Mayer/Star File • 33 (top) Kreitem/Rex USA, Kevin Mazur/London Features

TRIALS & TRIBULATIONS 34 Reuters/Bettmann • 35 (left) Gamma Liaison, Scott Downie/Celebrity Photo • 36 (top) Pool/Gamma Liaison, Ken Lubas/Los Angeles Times Photo • 37 (top) Globe Photos, Sygma • 38 (top) Kevin Winter/DMI, AP/ Wide World • 39 Larry Downing/Sygma • 40 Intersport Television • 41 (left) Brent Wojahn/The Oregonian/Sygma, Ed Hille/The Philadelphia Inquirer • 42 (top) Tom Treick/The Oregonian/Sygma, Sygma • 43 Andrew Renault/Globe • 44 (both) John Storey • 45 Bob Noble/Globe • 46 Neal Preston/Outline • 47 (both) San Francisco Chronicle/Sygma

SAVIORS & SURVIVORS 48 (top) David Leeson/Dallas Morning News/JB Pictures, John Storey • 50 Mariella Furrer • 51 Alexandra Boulat/Sipa • 52-53 (clockwise from top right) Jamie Razuri/Agence France-Presse, David Murray Jr./New York Times, Reuters/Bettmann, Robert Trippett/Sipa • 54 Eli Reed/Magnum • 55 Lori Grinker/Contact

WINNERS & LOSERS 56-57 © Michael Jacobs • 58 (left) James Smeal/Ron Galella, Bonnie Schiffman/Onyx • 59 Timothy White/Onyx • 60 (top) E.J. Carr/CBS, Bill Morris/ABC • 61 (top) Kevin Mazur, Frank Micelotta/Outline• 62 (top) Brian Smith/Outline, Diana Walker/Gamma Liaison • 63 Walter Iooss Jr. • 64 (top) Mike Powell/Allsport, Shaun Botterill/Allsport • 65 (top) Clive Brunskill/Allsport, Stephen Ellison/Outline • 66 (clockwise from top) Theo Westenberger, P.F. Bentley for Time, John Iacono/Sports Illustrated • 67 (top) AP/Wide World, Andrea Renault/Globe • 68 (top) AP/Wide World, James Kelly/Globe • 69 (top to bottom) Andy Gomperz/The Desert Sun, Brad Markel/Gamma Liaison, AP/Wide World

PARTINGS 70 (left) Miguel/Alpha/Globe, Alpha/Globe • 72 David Hartley/Rex USA • 73 (top) Derry Moore/Camera Press London/Retna, I. Burns/Camera Press/Globe • 74 (top to bottom) Albert Ferreira/DMI, Scott Downie/Celebrity Photo, Ramey Photo Agency • 75 (clockwise from top) Nikki Vai/Celebrity Photo, John Paschal/Celebrity Photo, Vincent Zuffante/Star File • 76 (top) Jeff Slocomb/Outline, Kevin Winter/DMI • 77 (top) Kelly Jordon/Celebrity Photo, A. Berliner/Gamma Liaison • 78 (top) A. Savignano/Ron Galella, Jeffrey Mayer/Star File • 79 (clockwise from top) Frank Micelotta/Retna, Tony Esparza/CBS, King/Gamma Liaison • 80 (clockwise from top) James Schnepf/Gamma Liaison, Tony Esparza/CBS, Clive Brunskill/Allsport • 81 (top) Paul Hosefros/NYT Pictures, Howell/Gamma Liaison

LOOK OF THE YEAR 82-83 Douglas Kirkland/Sygma • 84 (clockwise from top) Steve Granitz/Retna, Raeanne Rubenstein, Frank Trapper/Sygma • 85 (clockwise from top right) Robert Fairer/Retna, Colin Mason/London Features, Barbara Rosen/Images • 86 (top) Andrew Eccles/Edge, Steve Finn/Alpha/Globe • 87 Peggy Sirota/Outline

FAMILY MATTERS 88 Niviere/Villard/Sipa Press • 90-91 (clockwise from top right) Jim McHugh/Outline, Steve Sands/Outline, AP/Wide World, Albert Ferreira/DMI, Neil Gruhn/LGI • 92 (top to bottom) Alan L. Mayor, Mark Scott/LGI, John Paschal/Celebrity Photo • 93 (top) Joseph DeValle, no credit • 94 (top to bottom) Albert Ferreira/DMI, Fred Prouser/Sipa Press, Andrew Dunsmore/Rex USA • 95 Christian Durocher/Sygma • 96 (top to bottom) Edie Baskin/Onyx, M. Gerber/LGI, Big Pictures/Star File • 97 (top) David Walberg/Sports Illustrated, Ron Slenzak/King World • 98 (top) Ann States/Saba, David Strick/Onyx • 99 (top) Bill Frakes/Sports Illustrated, Courtesy Jive Records

GOODBYES 100-101 Ed Sirrs/Retna • 102 (top) Mimi Cotter, Photofest • 103 Aaron Rapoport/Onyx • 104 (top) Photofest, David Strick/Onyx • 105 Earl Wilson/Archive • 106 (top) Photofest, AP/Wide World • 107 Photofest • 108 Tony Korody/Sygma • 109 Brian Aris/Camera Press/Archive • 110 (top) Photofest, Anthony Crickway/Camera Press/Globe • 111 Photofest • 112 (top) Express Newspapers/Archive, Photofest • 113 G. Mathieson/Sygma • 114 (top) Photofest, David Gahr • 115 UPI/Bettmann • 116 (top) Graphic House, Steve Schapiro/Gamma Liaison • 117 Pat Harbron/Outline • 118 Harry Benson • 119 Howard Sochureck/ Life • 120 (top) Edie Baskin/Onyx, David Gahr • 121 Doc Pele/Stills/Retna • 122 (top) Paul Natkin/Photo Reserve, Dana Fineman/Sygma • 123 Archive • 124 (top) Frank Fishbeck, Photofest • 125 Ken Probst/Outline • 126 Photofest • 127 Archive • 128 (top) Photofest, Gerald Davis/Photoreporters • 129 Archive • 130 (top) Photofest, Kansas City Star/Sipa Press • 131 Tony Costa/Outline • 132 (top) From the Collection of Elizabeth Glaser, AP/Wide World • 133 Courtesy Henry Mancini Family • 134 (top) Lester Glassner Collection/Neal Peters, Jim McHugh/Outline • 135 Archive • 136-137 © The Mark Shaw Collection/Photo Researchers • 138 (clockwise from top right) UPI/Bettmann, © The Mark Shaw Collection/Photo Researchers, The Washington Post • 139 Fred Ward/Black Star • 140 (clockwise from top) Settimio Garritano/ Gamma Liaison, Keith Butler/Rex USA, Brian Quigley/Outline, Rick Friedman/Black Star • 141 © 1976 by Ron Galella from the book *Offguard* (McGraw-Hill)

INDEX